ONE PLAY MANY WAYS

TEACHING CONCEPTUAL FOOTBALL

Author: Kenny Simpson
Copyright
ISBN: 978-1-7351591-9-5

Being a coach has been a dream job for me for many years. I've never felt like it was work because I have felt this is what I was supposed to be doing. While there have been difficult seasons and great seasons, I've always felt this is what I was called to do for my profession.

Then, I began putting out coaching materials, and my focus began to shift. Now I was able to impact more people on a global scale. It was never my intention at the beginning of this journey to become an author and travel around to work with coaches, but it has been such a blessing.

That calling can be tough on those around you. It takes a special lady to be a coach's wife and I am blessed with the best one I could have asked for in Jamey. She has invested in my programs as much as I have and become a mother to many young athletes. Without her, I would have never been successful in this endeavor.

It also takes very patient children that understand their father cannot be there as much as he would like to be. I have three great children that have been a blessing in Avery, Braden and Bennett.

If anyone knows me personally, they know I would need a great editor that can clean up my writing. Having a mother-in-law that taught English has been a must! Thank you very much to Kay Jones for all her work editing many of my books.

Of course my own mother has been supportive and is the epitome of "football mom". Her encouragement has been there my entire life and hasn't stopped in this new journey.

INTRODUCTION

Introduction

A few years ago, I released my first book into the coaching world. I was hopeful it may sell 50 copies. The goal was simply to write a book and see it through. The response was more than I could have ever imagined.

Connecting with coaches across the globe has been one of my passions ever since that first book. If after reading this book, you'd like to connect, I'd be honored to talk about this or whatever you'd like. Thank you for the support of my materials. It is an honor to be able to hopefully share some knowledge with the coaching community.

This book is a continuation of a thought process I began a few seasons ago when I attempted to see an easier way to teach football. I touched on the subject in an earlier book, *Coaching Football Like A Basketball Coach*. It is my hope that this book continues in that thought process and adds some clarity and depth to thinking **conceptually** about the game of football.

When I think of offensive football in today's game, I attempt to think of **conceptual** football. Each play is fluid and needs to be able to adapt to take advantage of the weakness in the defense. What I mean by fluid, is the ability to take advantage of what the defense gives. Instead of a hard fast, we will do "X", and the offense should adjust and do "Y", if it is the better option. As you read through this book, it is my hope that you will find multiple ideas that illustrate this point much more clearly.

Introduction

The premise of this entire book is that an offensive system built from **conceptual plays** will be versatile, yet simple for the players.

For example, in many systems an offense will run "36 lead" as a play. If the defense aligns perfectly to stop this run, they have a few rules to help, but are pretty much tied to running the "3" back through the "6" hole. If they want to run the ball with another back or run it a hole tighter, they will simply change the play. If they were teaching this as a **concept** it could be called "Iso" or "Blast" or whatever the coach chooses for the **concept**. The rules of the **concept** would dictate the hole the offense wanted to attack based on the alignment of the defense. The runner could be tagged to anyone in the backfield. This allows for an offense to have a more fluid streamlined look that takes advantage of what is presented by the defense instead of a rigid system that can become wordy or difficult to understand.

Another benefit of teaching through **concepts** is that when players understand the **concept** of each play, they will be able to make quick adjustments. When the team understands what the goal is, they will feel a vested interest in understanding the "how" and "why". This helps the offensive coordinator by keeping the offense on the same page, but it also creates "buy-in" from the players.

Introduction

This entire book will follow the premise of making the offensive system very versatile, and yet simple. While it takes a little time on the front end, the goal would be to become so well versed in the play **concept** that it will be successful against any front or any coverage. Instead of allowing a defense to take away a **concept**, the offense goes to an adjustment that is built into the play.

I hope you can take some of this type of thinking into your own offensive system. I will use 3 base run plays and 3 types of pass plays as an example in this book, but the goal is to take the same thought process and use it in any offense with any play.

If you would like to see my specific offense

Table of Contents

Forward	11
Teaching Concepts, Not Plays	15
Think Like A Defensive Coordinator	27
RPO Concepts	39
Using Motion	49
'The Blend"	61
Common Mistakes	75
Run Game Section	83
Buck	87
ISO	107
Counter	123
Pass Game Section	141
Rollout	143
Play Action	153
Screens	163
Conclusion	171
About the Author	175

FORWARD

Forward

I first became aware of who Coach Kenny Simpson was when he became the Head Football Coach at my high school alma mater, Alabama Christian Academy, in Montgomery, Alabama in 2008. My alma mater had struggled in football and Coach Simpson made some noticeable progress with the program. However, it wasn't until our two schools were placed in the same conference in 2014 in Arkansas, that we began to have more interaction and discussion about the sport for which we both share a passion. When Coach Simpson took over the Southside program, it was a program that had not experienced much success. Most years Southside was not competitive within their own conference, much less at the state level.

When Southside first joined our conference they continued to struggle to experience success. Beginning with our first contest in 2014, Coach Simpson would always seek feedback on how he could improve his program. We would often exchange game plan information and scouting reports. It was not uncommon for me to receive a call asking for insights into our common opponents. It became apparent to me from the detail included in their scouting reports, that Coach Simpson and his staff had put a tremendous amount of time and effort into preparing their team.

Forward

Over time, the fruit of that hard work has begun showing up on the scoreboard. Coach Simpson and Southside High School have gone from being a team that many likely overlooked to a team that competes for the conference championship on a yearly basis.

The building of the program at Southside by Coach Simpson and his staff has certainly been impressive. Those efforts have produced teams that are well prepared and play with discipline and great effort. I also believe that much of that success can be tied directly to the unique style of offense that Coach Simpson has implemented and evolved in his time at Southside. The offensive system that Coach Simpson and his staff have put into use is a perfect fit for their athletes. More importantly, their players believe in it because they've begun experiencing success.

Outside of just having better players than your opponent, I believe there are a few core traits that produce a successful offensive system. An offensive system should be simple enough that athletes can execute at a high level. This system would also allow athletes to play fast and with confidence in their assignments. At the same time, within that simplicity, the offense should give the appearance of complexity and have built in answers to the defensive approach of our opponent.

Forward

The principles that Coach Simpson describes in this book address those needs and can help coaches in formulating a plan to make their offense more successful. I believe that readers will find the principles within this book to be sound, well laid out, and applicable to any style or system of offensive football. So, whether you are new to the coaching profession, or a veteran coach looking to learn like myself, you will find some nuggets in this book that can help you.

Tommy Shoemaker
Head Football Coach
Central Arkansas Christian

CHAPTER 1

TEACHING CONCEPTS

Teaching Concepts

*"If you can't explain it simply,
you don't understand it well enough."*
Albert Einstein

A **concept** is not just a play, but it is an idea for a fluid play in football. A play that allows for adjustments by the players and coaches. A **concept** is a larger idea than just running "34 dive" or "shallow cross". It is seeing the game and teaching the game as adjustable instantly based on what a defense does.

When a coach calls a play – for example 34 dive, he is limiting our offense to hand the ball to the "3" back through the "4" hole, or however the offense call plays. This type of offense relies on the offense opening a hole in the "B" gap of the defense and relies on the running back to always carry out the play. If they want to run the ball a gap wider, it will need to become a different play. Or, if they want to hand the ball off to another runner, it becomes a different play.

When we look at this same play as a "**concept**" we would teach it as more of a fluid and adjustable idea. Instead of "34 dive", we may call it simply "dive". We teach our offensive line that we want the play to hit in the A, B, or C gap, but teach them all the "ifs" that would make the play adjust. Then we teach that the base **concept** would be to hand the ball to the running back, but we can tag or adjust the ball carrier by simply adding a word.

Teaching Concepts

The **concept** then becomes much more fluid and adjustable for the offense. This should allow it to be successful regardless of what the defense shows. Running a rules-based offense has been around for decades and is a great start. The next step is to begin to teach the "why" for the rules.

Concepts require teaching the players the "why" of the play. What are we attempting to do? How will we adjust to different looks? What techniques will work for this concept to be successful? What will we do when the defense does _____? These and additional questions must be asked and answered for any **concept** that will be run in the offensive system.

This is very much in the "If-Then" thought process. Working through this process will help you as a coach, but also your athletes learn what is needed. This should allow everyone to know the offense in depth. Any **concept** that is put in the offense must be thoroughly explored and studied. While this will technically "shrink the playbook", it will cause each **concept** that is installed to be adjustable and thoroughly understood.

When a team understands the **concept** and the ultimate goal of what the team is trying to achieve, they are able to help make quick adjustments to make the **concept** successful. This allows for a smaller, but more understood playbook.

Teaching Concepts

Instead of having multiple plays that must all be studied and installed, the offense has fewer **concepts** that, when adjusted, appear to a defense as a much more complex system.

This has become the norm now of many spread football teams that run "read" routes. It is also becoming used much more even inside of how a route is taught. For example: we teach a wide receiver running a "go" route that if he is "capped", or unable to get over the defender, then he will break off his route and convert it into a "stop" route. Or, we teach the quarterback to throw the ball to his back shoulder. In each scenario, we are teaching the **concept** of the play and how to make the adjustments needed to be successful. This has been called a "VR" or vertical release route in many offensive systems. The receiver releases and reads the leverage of the defense.

Great offenses will do this with every play they run. And great offensive coordinators do this by understanding how to call the right formation, adjustment and of course play. It is my hope that reading through this book gives a few small examples of how teaching **concepts** over plays will lead to a much higher understanding by your players, and in-turn create a much more efficient offensive system.

Teaching Concepts

Once a coach and his players see the game as fluid and build a system that allows for quick adjustments, it makes playing the actual game much easier. Instead of having "this plan" for a cover 2 team and "that plan" for a cover 3 team, a coach now builds in his adjustments on the front end. When the players understand how they will adjust each **concept,** it allows for a team to play with confidence and for the playbook to shrink in number of plays, as each "**concept**" may look like 4-5 "plays".

Conceptual teaching is nothing new to many coaches, as it has been around for a long period of time. For example, many spread teams have been teaching "choice" routes for years, based on the leverage of the defender. The wide receiver has a choice pre-snap of which route to run.

In a "choice" route, a receiver is given a choice of 3-4 routes that he can pick from based on coverage. If the defensive player is playing off, he may run a hitch. If he is playing outside leverage he can run a slant/post. If it is press-man coverage it may be a go route.

Then it was taken a step further. Now, many routes have post-snap reads. The wide receiver has a go, unless he is "capped", as was stated in the previous page. The players are now learning how to adjust to the defense within the **concept** being run.

Teaching Concepts

Giving freedom to the players that are making the decisions based on what the defense shows is a great way to make sure the offense will have built in answers.

This is teaching the player a **concept**, teaching him how to react to the defense and how to adjust based on what he is seeing. When an offense begins to teach players **concepts**, they will be more confident in the system. This takes some time on the front end, but it ensures that players understand what is the goal of each **concept**.

Doing this with the offensive line has become a part of football as well. A great example of this is the pin-and-pull game. Teaching linemen that all uncovered linemen will pull to the play side and those covered will block the defensive linemen is much more of a **concept** than simply a play.

The older way to teach this would have been to tell "X" player he was pulling and "Y" player he was blocking the defensive linemen. And if the defense shifted from the predicted front...there were problems. Now, teaching them the overall **concept** of the play, the linemen can think for themselves and communicate the adjustments.

While we teach our base rules of blocking and make it simple for the offensive line, we also teach the potential adjustments, or the "If-Then" situations. This helps the players understand what we are attempting to achieve and gives them the ability to think for themselves. It has reaped tremendous benefits in our offensive system.

Teaching Concepts

This should also allow for the ability to run the same **concept** with multiple players. For example, this book will cover running the buck sweep concept. If taught to the team as a **concept**, we should be able to run the ball with our running back, quarterback, slotback or even another player by simply tagging them into the play.

When teaching **concepts**, it will take more time on the front end. It is important that each player understands what the goal is, issues that will need to be addressed, adjustments that need to be made against different looks and so forth. However, once the concept is taught, it will be very adaptable. Simply put, teaching **concepts** allows for an offense to drastically shrink their "plays", but have so much flexibility that to a defense it seems they have multiple looks.

The entire goal of this book is to show a few examples of how to implement this type of teaching. Great coaches can run the Air Raid, Wing T, Option or any type of offensive system. What makes these offenses excel is that the system has built in **concepts** and adjustments. While this book will focus on concepts that I have personally run, the same thought process can be applied to all types of offenses, or even defensive systems.

I do want to caution that teaching **concepts** and not plays will take much more time and depth from the coach. This will mean a coach will need to "trim" his playbook and limit his team to less **concepts**.

Teaching Concepts

To become great at a **concept**, a team will need to understand the "why" behind it. They will also need to be able to understand potential adjustments and counters a defense will throw at them to stop it.

Once I go through this further in detail in this book it will not appear to be a small playbook since each can adapt. Take the time up-front to teach the **concept** in as much depth as possible and it will be worth it. The rest of this book will walk through the importance of being immersed in a **concept**.

Teams that are successful use the phrase:

"This is the same as _____, with this adjustment".

In the next few pages there will be an example of how we use the **concept** of Buck Sweep. If we teach this **concept** correctly, it will allow us to dress it up, and when the base rules are taught, the **concept** will be more fluid than the old-school "26 buck sweep".

Teaching Concepts

I will be using Buck Sweep as our example for each chapter. Do not think this is the "only" **concept** you can apply this line of thinking towards. It should be in every **concept** you install in an offensive system. This is simply an example of this type of thinking.

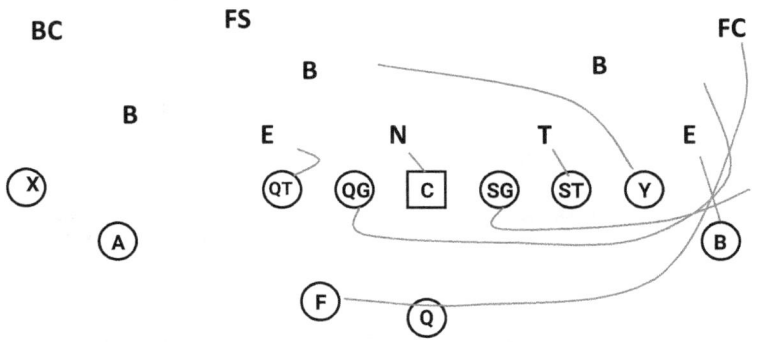

Position	Assignment
X	RPO Called
A	RPO Called
F	Cross QB Face – Stay Horizontal 3 Steps – Follow Guard
Y	Gap-Down-Backer
B	Gap-Down-Backer
QT	Gap-Hinge – Unless RPO Tag is Used
QG	Pull Wrap
C	On-Backside
SG	Pull Kick
ST	Gap-Down-Backer
Q	RPO Read

Teaching Concepts
Buck Rules

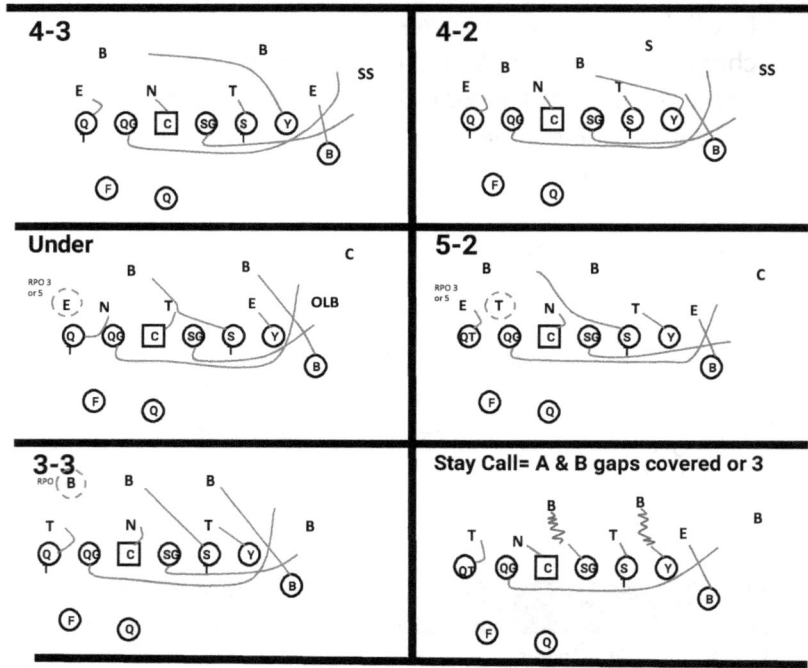

These are just a few examples of the fronts a runner must be prepared to face. When teaching **concepts** most teams will be "rules-based". For buck sweep the rule is "gap-down-backer" on the play side.

This allows for the linemen to simply follow their rules, and they should be able to pick up any front that the defense will show. It may not be the optimal way to block the front, but the rules make is simple and clear.

The **concept** is fluid and not a hard and fast "hole and number". The goal is to be flexible and take advantage of the defense.

Teaching Concepts

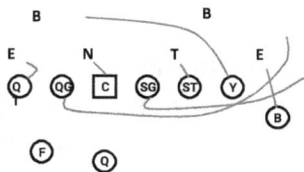

When teaching the base rules of buck sweep, the front should not matter. That is why teaching **concepts** should allow for an easily adjustable front. For this specific front:

Wing has the 9 technique – he is "in his gap"
Y has the backside LB – he is "backer"
Tackle has the 3 technique – he is "in his gap"
Guards pull
Backside Tackle will step-hinge

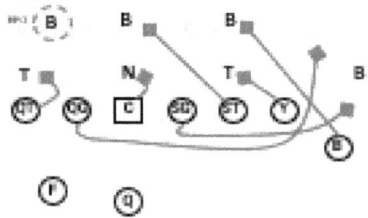

In this front:
Wing blocks LB – his rule is "gap-down-backer", since no defensive lineman is in his gap or down, he has LB
Y – blocks "down"
Tackle – blocks "backer"
Guards pull
Backside Tackle will step-hinge
In this front – the backside linebacker is unaccounted for, so the QB must read him

Teaching Concepts

This will be explored further in detail in this book. Once applied to a playbook with few **concepts**, it will not appear to be a small playbook since each can adapt. Take the time up-front to teach the **concept** in as much depth as possible and it will be worth it. The rest of this book will walk through the importance of being immersed in a **concept**.

Remember, teams that are successful use the phrase:

"This is the same as _____, with this adjustment".

Most offensive systems have moved to teaching rules-based blocking schemes. As the book progresses, it should show that when the team understands the depth of the **concept**, making quick adjustments will be simple.

"Spoon-feeding, in the long run, teaches us nothing but the shape of the spoon"
E. M. Forster

CHAPTER 2

THINK LIKE A DEFENSIVE COORDINATOR

Think Like A Defensive Coordinator

"We don't see things as they are, we see them as we are."
Anais Nin

I cut my teeth as a defensive line coach, then a defensive backs' coach and finally as a defensive coordinator before becoming a head coach. To me this was such a blessing as I have transitioned over to the offensive side of the ball. Learning how a defense functions and how it sets up keys to stop an offense is a MUST for great offensive minds. It is almost like I was able to see what would be on the test, before I took it.

As you design your offense it is imperative that you see it through the lens of a defensive coordinator. Some coaches call this "self-scout" and others call it "padding", but it is essential to a great offense that you understand how a defense will attack your offense. There are certain rules defenses will install that can be used against them. This chapter will explore a few of them, and once a coach studies the opponent, these will become clear and help his offense.

In order to run a high functioning offense, a coach must understand the basic principles of a defense. Studying defensive techniques and terminology will always allow an offensive coach to understand what he is up against. Defenses will adapt each year as well to match-up with offenses, and a coach must understand the adjustments.

Think Like A Defensive Coordinator

Not only must a coach understand the basic principles of the defense, but they must see their offense through the eyes of a defensive coordinator. Where will they attack the formation? What player will the game plan stop? Who is the defense hiding? What checks have they shown in the past to trips, empty, two-tight and more?

Once an offensive coordinator has the answers to these questions, then the chess match can begin. For a coach to gain many of these answers will require hours of film study. It will also require some planning early in the game to confirm what the answers were.

Example #1
When scouting a defense, you may notice they always check to a certain coverage when the offense shows trips. In our first few plays, we will align in trips to confirm the defense is doing what we expected based on film. If they do, we should have our game plan ready. If they do not, we must understand why they are treating our offense differently than previous ones.

Do they have different personnel in the game? Do they feel we can/can not pass the ball? Why would they show a different look against our team?

These are the types of questions we should be asking if we are seeing our offense through the eyes of a defensive coordinator.

Think Like A Defensive Coordinator

Example #2
When scouting a defense, you may notice they call strength to the tight end. This is common in most defensive structures, but when you dig deeper you may realize they are also playing a "strong" side of the defensive line to that call or simply slanting to the call.

To test this theory out quickly, an offense may choose to line up with a tight end in the first few plays and monitor if the defense does what it has shown all season and move their personnel to match the strong side. If they do this, the game plan that is prepared should be good to go. The offense can move the strength of the formation to take advantage of the smaller players on the weak side, or they may line up the tight end away from where they want to run the ball.

If the defense does not line up as predicted, the offense must again ask why. Does the offense have a tendency to run weak? Do they view our tight end as more of a receiving threat? Are they attempting to remain balanced in their strength?

Once the questions are answered, we will tweak the game plan to match what the defense is giving.

Think Like A Defensive Coordinator

To get the point across without going into a full book on the "If-Then" ideology, here are a few simple ones to consider:

If the defense is loading the box, **Then** we will _____.

If the defense is playing man to man, **Then** we will _____.

If the defense is blitzing and moving, **Then** we will _____.

If the defense is playing off coverage, **Then** we will _____.

If the defense is committed to stopping our ____ player, **Then** we will _____.

Using this type of thinking will allow an offense to build in answers to its full system. The next progression is taking this to each **concept** that is built into the offense. In
upcoming chapters this book will dive into a few examples of how this type of thinking must happen with each **concept** of offense runs.

A well-designed offense will think through as many "If-Then" answers as possible. Having a built-in plan of attack for anticipated defensive alignments, blitzes and coverages is the mark of a well-designed system. Be sure to take this thought process throughout, not only each **concept** that is installed, but how each **concept** will be complemented with counters, formations, motions, etc...

Think Like A Defensive Coordinator

Defensive coaches will also look for areas to attack an offense. They will find your weakness and exploit it. As an offensive coordinator you must be very self-aware of what your film shows. Not what you may personally know, but what is showing up on film. The defensive teams scouting you will look to see what has proven to be successful against your offense in the past and will attempt to use that strategy.

Most teams refer to this as self-scouting when looking at your offense, but through the eyes of a defensive coordinator. Obviously, running the reports of how many tendencies you have is important, but also looking at what players you have that are creating big plays, and how you are using them. They will set a defense to stop this.

This means in your offensive system you must build in "If-Then" **concepts** to counter what a defense will potentially do. Many offenses, mine included, do this through the RPO game, or running the same backfield action for play action or counters. But the great offenses are able to also use the tags for blocking to continue running the same play with different adjustments.

Teach the concepts to players in terms they can understand. Some players can handle more, and some will need to slowly be brought along. It will take more time on the front end, but it will be worth it long-term.

Think Like A Defensive Coordinator

Defensive coaches also have tendencies like offensive coaches. When breaking down the opponent's defense, I'd ask the following questions:

1) Are they relying on movement and stunts, or are they relying on technique and more stationary pre-snap?

1) Do they have a base coverage and adjustment? When and how often do they change that coverage?

1) When do they change to a goal-line, short yardage package? What do they attempt to do in that package?

1) Do they have a player they are attempting to "hide"? How are they compensating for his weakness?

1) Do they have a dominant player? How are they using him to showcase his ability?

1) Do they adjust to boundary and field calls? Do they stick to formation adjustments? (Basically, if you play trips to the boundary, how will they handle that call).

1) Do they adjust to overloads or unbalanced looks?

1) How do they handle motion?

Think Like A Defensive Coordinator

Using Buck Sweep as our example, here is how the "IF-THEN" thought process would look:

IF the defense overloads to stop Buck Sweep

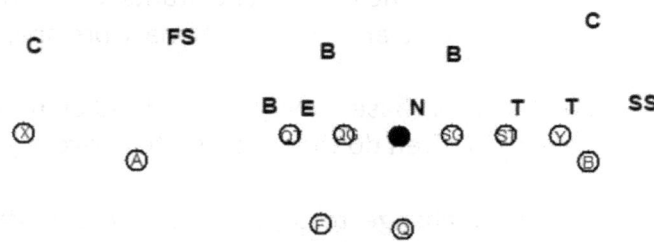

THEN

1) ISO – Block out on Defensive line and run underneath SS

1) Strong side play action – Read the corner for the shot play

1) B-Pop or X Crack and go – If corner is very aggressive make the read simple for your QB

1) Waggle – More than likely TE will come wide open in this look

1) RPO Game on the backside – Steal would be a good call here for QB pull. Could also just throw quick game depending on depth of DB's

1) Counter – Counter is also an option in this look

Think Like A Defensive Coordinator

IF we are not able to get movement against a 9 Technique

THEN

1) Run "bypass" and kick him out if he is an up-field penetrating defensive player.

1) Have the TE base him for 1-count before releasing inside on buck sweep.

1) Widen his splits by alignment.

1) Run "trade" and move your TE/Wing away from him pre-snap.

As you work through the buck sweep more in depth you will find other issues that must be addressed. This book is not meant to be an in-depth study of buck sweep, but simply showing how each part of the **concept** must be planned for and taught to the athletes.

If you would like more depth on the buck sweep there are multiple materials available at FBCoachsimpson.com.

Think Like A Defensive Coordinator

Once an offensive coordinator has a basic idea of the structure of the defense, he can begin to see how his **concepts** will adjust (or how he predicts they will adjust). This should allow for a gameplan to be formulated. While the offense could simply run its base **concepts** and make in-game adjustments, doing research on the defense will help to create the matchups desired.

Before implementing a **concept**, an offensive system must see the strengths and weakness of each **concept** through the eyes of a defensive coordinator and build in answers to any situation, but especially potential problems a defense can cause. Again, this will take a significant amount of time, and it will limit how many **concepts** an offense can run. This is a good thing. Become great at each **concept**.

Using formations and RPO's are great, but they are useless if an offensive coordinator doesn't understand how to manipulate the defensive structure to isolate a player for the RPO, or how to use a formation to create a +1 for the offense. Seeing the game through the eyes of a defensive coordinator will help to clarify why formations and RPO's are such a problem. Just like on offense, any scheme a defensive team will throw out has strengths and weaknesses. It is up to the offensive coordinator to find those and expose them, and that can only happen if he understands defensive systems.

Think Like A Defensive Coordinator

This will take quite a bit of time on the front end. That is why I would recommend speaking to coaches that have been running a similar system to what you may decide to run. These coaches have already had to answer problems a defense threw at them in the game. They will be able to tell you areas their offensive system struggled, and what they hope to do to fix those issues. Speaking and learning from coaches is the best way to gain insight as a play caller.

When a coach views his offense from an outside perspective – or a defensive coordinator's viewpoint – it should help him to see the adjustments that must be built into the **concept**. A **concept** should never be abandoned because a defense aligns a certain way, or runs a certain coverage. While some **concepts** are better against different looks, they should always be able to function regardless of the defense if the adjustments are built-in to the **concept**.

"What is behind your eyes holds more power than what is in front of them."
Gary Zukav

CHAPTER 3

RPO CONCEPTS

RPO Concepts

"RPO is the purest form of communism"
Pat Fitzgerald

Coach Fitzgerald is not alone in his distaste for the RPO game. Many coaches, usually defensive minded coaches, have shared how much they dislike this offense. The reason...it is hard to stop if run correctly. Working through the levels of the RPO protects the run game by always keeping good numbers. It also sets up very simple and easy passes for the quarterback.

The term RPO has revolutionized football at the high school and college level. It is now becoming much more used at the NFL level. That said, this is not a new **concept** anymore. For those new to this world, RPO simply is a play that is designed for the quarterback to have options in the run game and passing/screen game **after** the snap.

While there are many "divorced concepts" – or a run play with a pre-snap read for a pass – that are great options for an offense, this book will not cover those **concepts.** They are great for any offense to have and have been around for a long time. These would consist generally of a screen pass or single WR route that the QB can choose pre-snap and throw at any time. This book will instead focus on true RPO's, or plays that are tied together and read post-snap.

RPO Concepts

There are hundreds of books dedicated to the RPO game. To keep things as simple as possible, this book will focus on the "why" of the RPO that can be installed into an offensive system. Fortunately, the why is actually pretty simple for most offensive coaches... answering problems. That is the number one goal of all systems, and the RPO system is no different.

Here is how an RPO answers problems for an offense:

Picking on a conflict defender
Generally, most RPOs are designed to make a specific defender wrong. The easiest ways to do this would be to have the quarterback read the defender to pull and run (RRO), or pull the ball and throw to a wide receiver running in the vacated area.

As a coach, you are only limited in your RPO selection by your own imagination. Working to have multiple tags to read different defenders on each run **concept** should be the goal. As you build an offense, the goal would be to tag all of the "problem areas" when running a play. That could be the backside linebacker, an overhang defender or even a defensive lineman. These are defenders that the offense wants to put in conflict. Make them wrong regardless of what they do.

RPO Concepts

Putting the quarterback in a simple "If-Then"

"If-Then" football makes things very simple on any player. In the RPO game, it cleans up where the quarterback looks before and after the snap. It becomes a simple IF the read does "X", THEN we do "Y".

While this book will walk through a few different flavors of RPOs, the offense is only limited to what the coach and the quarterback are able to do. Teaching the quarterback is essential to success in the RPO world. The simplest form of RPO would be a pre-snap read, followed by a read of a defensive lineman and then a read of a second level defender.

As the quarterback and coach become more comfortable, the RPO game can expand to a two-part read... reading a defensive lineman to a second level defender, or it can change to reading a defensive back. The possibilities are almost limitless.

While this may take some time to install in your offense, it keeps the game very simple for a quarterback. Instead of asking them to read an entire defense, often they are simply looking at one defensive player after the ball is snapped. This makes playing quarterback much simpler than having to read through full progressions. It takes a large understanding by the coach, but is actually very simple for the quarterback and players.

RPO Concepts

Allowing the offense to gain numbers
When an offense is able to use RPOs, they will now be able to gain the numbers in the running or passing game. By leaving players unblocked and reading them, the offense can always account for the defensive scheme and have enough blockers to make the running game work. RPOs have evolved over the years, but most coaches think they originated from the same mindset as option football. Instead of reading only to run and pitch, now they read to hand the ball off or pass.

The entire premise of many offenses is to attempt to get +1 in the running game. The ability to leave a player that would normally be a problem in the run game unblocked, and to simply read him with either a route behind him or the QB pulling to run the ball has fundamentally changed the running game of all shotgun offenses. If taken to another level, the offense can dictate the defensive player they do not block by building in tags to read each position and then game planning to read the best defensive player each week or possession.

Many defenses will counter this by playing man-to-man coverage. While this does kill many RPOs to the receivers, it can still be done with box players as what I refer to as an RRO – or Run-Run-Option. The quarterback either hands the ball off or pulls it depending on the bonus defensive player that is involved in the read.

RPO Concepts

Helping against very talented defenders
Another major reason to run RPOs is to make a player "wrong" on defense. Or, as many option teams will put it, to "read" this player and either hand the ball off or pull it out and possibly throw the ball. This is a very easy way to attempt to take a talented player out of the game.

The entire premise of the RPO game was to read players, and one way to do this is to design the RPO to read the player who poses the biggest threat to the offense. In this book we will discuss the "Blend", or using motion, formations and other factors to create better matchups for the offense. A talented offensive coordinator is able to use those tools to isolate the defensive player he wants to read in the RPO game. If done correctly, this can frustrate a great player on defense and lessen his impact on the game.

How ever a team chooses to use RPOs, the use of them helps assist the running game by creating an advantage for the offense. While many coaches shy away from the RPO game due to the feeling it is complex, it is actually a simple and quick installation. The ability to block as few players as possible helps the offense's ability to protect the running game against a stacked box.

RPO Concepts

Following this line of thinking we will use Buck Sweep as an example **concept**. Adding in the RPO element to help against potential issues a defense will throw out to stop the **concept**, the RPO element can solve many of the problems.

RPO Concepts

"Peak"
A works inside leverage, X a Post. QB Reads ILB

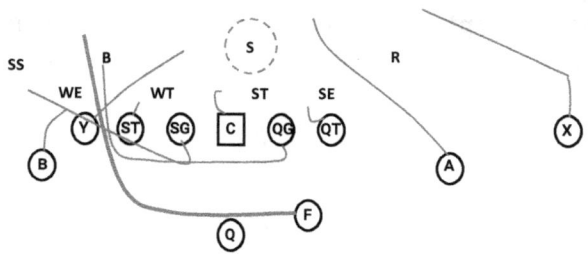

"Key"
Can throw fast screen (A steps on toes of "X" and blocks Most Dangerous). Post snap QB reads ILB for a run

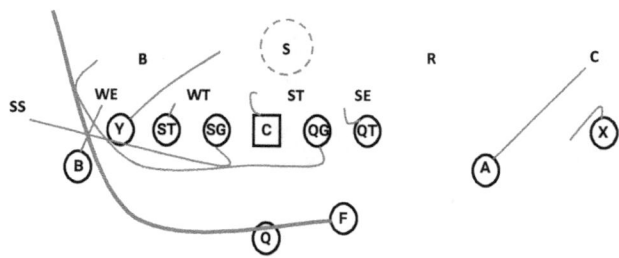

RPO Concepts

"Read and Bogo"
QB reads the 5 tech. Can throw bubble post snap

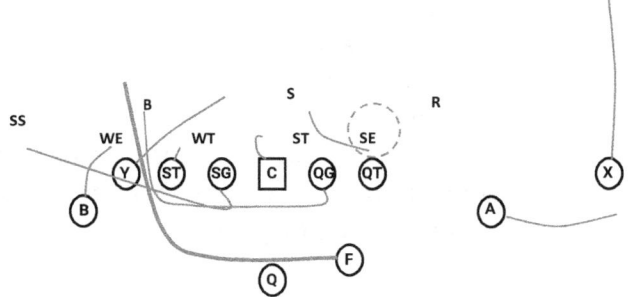

"Steal"
QB reads the 4i/3 tech

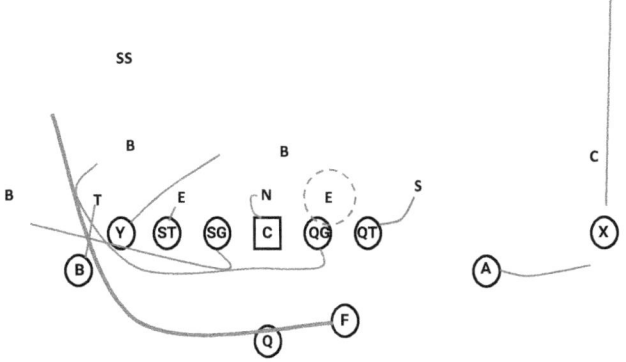

RPO Concepts

If an offense decides to use RPOs, there are many examples as they have become a staple in almost all shotgun offensive systems. This book will walk through a few RPOs used in my specific system, but the beauty about RPOs is that they can be added to any run and are only as limited as the ability of the offense to teach them. If your offensive system is heavily using the shotgun, it is a great weapon to add.

"To be creative, lose the fear of being wrong."
Unknown

CHAPTER 4

USING MOTION

Using Motion and Formation

"The shifts and motions are very specific to each play. There's a purpose to why we're doing it. We're not just shifting and motioning and running people all across the field just for the heck of it. There's a reason. We're trying to get an advantage. We're trying to outnumber them. We're trying to see a coverage or something."
Kellen Moore

One major area that some coaches show their ability to create the matchups and confusion they want is through motion and formations. The huge advantage for an offense over a defense is to set up the best possible matchup to achieve the desired outcome. As an offensive coordinator, the game is slanted to favor the offense since many offensive coordinators can use formations, shifts and motions to create the matchup or numbers advantage.

A good offensive system should have the ability to move any skill player through alignment, or to shift them with simple tags. While this can seem difficult for the coach as it creates multiple options, it is very simple for each player as they simply listen for their "tag" that moves them. Making an offense seem complex and thus causing it to be difficult to stop is the goal. Formations and motions are simply the tool to create the mismatch or numbers advantage.

Using Motion and Formation

While this phenomenon has been happening since the beginning of the game, only recently we are seeing this happen more and more. Here are a few key areas this shows up in football:

Creating a +1
Creating a great matchup
Creating an advantage for a player

In the rest of this chapter, I will explore those three major areas. The main goals for offense should be to accomplish one, two, or in a perfect scenario all three of those goals. If an offensive coordinator is able to consistently do this, he has put his team in a great position to succeed.

While there are many opportunities for an offense to create an advantage, formations and motions are the least expensive to install. Another way to make formations and shifts effective is to run them with tempo. Motion quickly before the snap or align in an unbalanced look and snap the ball quickly. Tempo and alignment should go hand and hand.

Another way to use tempo to help with formations is to use a "check with me" system. Align in a formation and use a dead count as the offense surveys how the defense plans to react to the set. Then a play-caller can call the best play to accomplish his goals.

Using Motion and Formation

Creating a +1
There are multiple ways an offense can use motion to get a bonus blocker to the point of attack in the run game, or a numbers advantage in the passing/screen game. The most simple way to do this, is to create an additional player at the point of attack, such as moving an H-back to gain an advantage in the running game. While this can also be done, post-snap by pulling him. It is often easier to move him from one side of the formation to another to gain numbers.

Another way to gain numbers is shifting a receiver from one side of the formation to another, or to shift a running back out to receiver right before the snap. This will create a decision for the defense. Do they shift with the receiver or attempt to run with them from across the formation? Either way an offense can run the same play they would have run, but by shifting a player they create an advantage.

There are two major ways to gain numbers through formations. One, is to bring more offensive players to one side of the field. The other, is to get the defense to over-commit to one side of the field and come back to the "weaker" side. If given a choice, that is the easier way to run an offense as it requires less players to execute their assignment to find success. While a 7 over 6 is a +1 for the offense, it still requires 6 players to execute. The "weak side" may have a 3 over 2 and simply requires 2 players to execute.

Using Motion and Formation

Creating a great matchup
One of the major goals for all offenses should be to create a 1-on-1 matchup for the best athlete. That matchup is even better if it is against a lesser athlete on the defensive side of the ball. Formations and motioning can help to create this matchup if used correctly. Once an offensive coordinator has identified the player on defense they would like to expose, the chess match has begun.

There are a multitude of ways to create this matchup. However, the starting point is to understand the basic rules of the defense. Are they passing motion off? Do they match up man-to-man with a single wide receiver or running back? What is the adjustment to an empty set? Do they matchup with players or positions?

Now, to walk through a few of these questions with some ideas.

Using motion is a quick way to create a good matchup. If the defense attempts to run with the motion, then the player can be run through traffic which will lead to several natural "rubs" or "picks". If the defense passes the player off, the offense can decide which matchup they prefer. If the player on the other side is considered a weaker player, the offense can motion each play to create the matchup they want.

Using Motion and Formation

Using formations to dictate that a defense plays man-to-man on the backside is also a tactic to create a great matchup. For example: if the defense always defends the backside receiver away from trips in man to man, the offense can put their best receiver as the single away from trips. Or, they can quickly motion a back out to the single receiver and create a matchup with a linebacker.

The same can be done if an offense recognizes the defense is playing man-to-man on the running back with linebackers. There are no rules that dictate having a receiver line up in the running back position to get the better matchup. If a defense is matching up with positions, it is a simple move to put the best offensive player at the most favorable position. This does mean the offensive players must understand the full **concept** as they may be playing a different position, but if they are able to do this, creating a great matchup is easier.

Another tactic is to line up in an empty set. Often defenses have 1-2 adjustments or rules to empty sets. Many times this will create either a light box (low numbers for empty running game) or man-to-man matchups. By finding the weaker defensive player, an offense can move their best athlete to create a favorable matchup. Or, if the defense shows the respect to that athlete, simply motioning a back into the backfield can create a good situation for the offense to run the ball against less numbers in the box.

Using Motion and Formation

Creating an advantage for a player
Creating matchups is great for an offense, but there will be times that a player may still struggle to win against a 1-on-1 matchup. Formations can also help to make the matchup more favorable. Using "bunch" formations or quick motions will often create space for an offensive player. This is a good way to keep him "clean" or make it difficult for a defense to get contact on him.

Another way to create an advantage for a player is to use splits. If a defense is playing a zone coverage and using an overhang player in run support, the offense can create issues by widening the splits of the wide receivers to create much more space for the defender to be responsible for. This can help define the defender's role, but it also makes it very difficult for the defense to ask the player to do two jobs, thus the definition of a "conflict defender".

On the following pages we will continue to use Buck Sweep as our example. Using motions and formations can help manipulate the defensive alignment and keys to help this **concept** be successful.

Using Motion and Formation

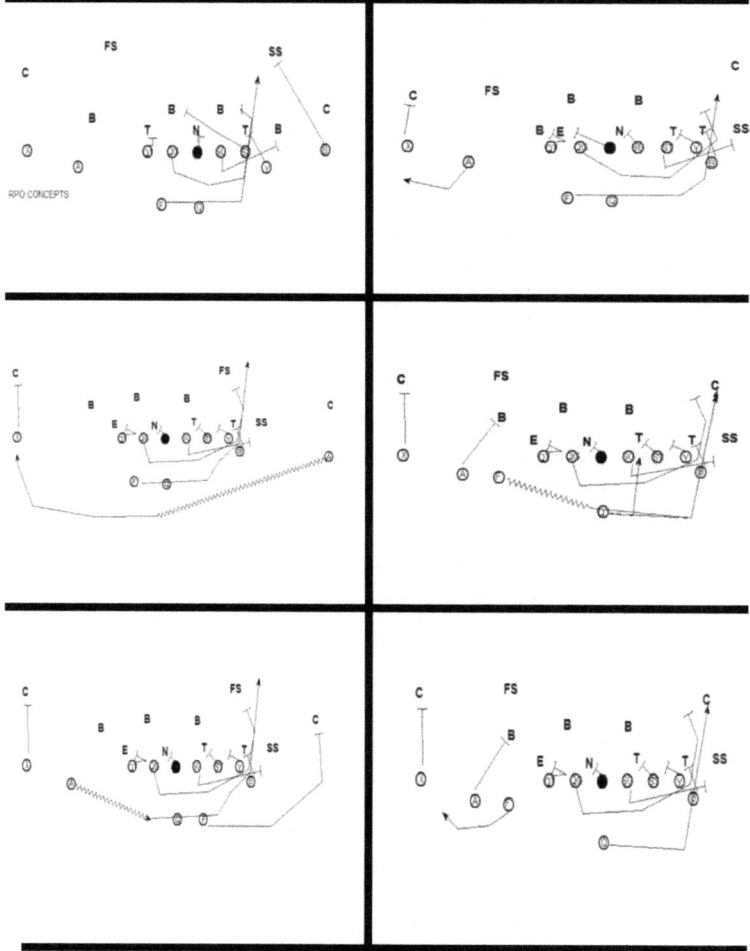

These are just a few examples using formations and motion to manipulate the defense into aligning how the offense wants them to. Using formations and then motions can create problems if used correctly.

Using Motion and Formation

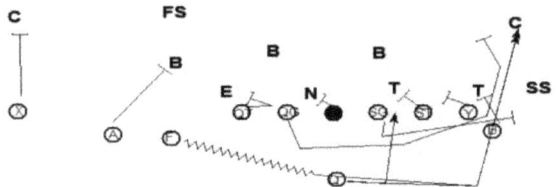

In the first example the offense aligns in an Empty set. Generally, this will cause the defense to get into a 2-high look or lighten the box. The offense then simply brings the same player in motion to run buck sweep. It changes nothing for any player, other than the motion, but to a defense it causes a lighter box and a quick adjusting safety or DB.

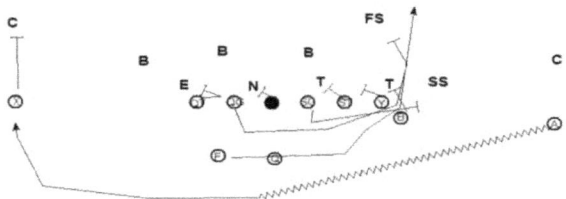

In this example the offense lines up in a Trips-Strong look. The use of motion (designed for a man-to-man team) will cause the defense problems as they have to either run with the motion, or roll the secondary.

In both plays the offense simply motioned players to create a problem for the defense and used formations to get the alignment they wanted.

Using Motion and Formation

Using formations in an offense is a very simple, but effective way to create great matchups for your team. It is also an under-utilized way to help offset when the opponent may have an advantage. While most of the focus for offensive coaches is to create matchups for their dominant players, often a coach must be able to avoid potential dominant defenders.

All defensive systems have built in rules for alignment. When an offensive coordinator understands how the defense will align to certain formations, he can now manipulate where the best defensive player will line up. The key to being able to accomplish all of this is to have built in tags for each player to move and shift. This seems like it would be very difficult, and it is for the coach, but not the players.

For example, if the best player lines up to what the defense declares the "strong" side of the offensive formation, a simple shift or pre-snap motion can change the formation and allow an offense to run the same play, but against a lesser defender. This can also be accomplished with moving wide receivers around pre-snap to create a better matchup. The goal of an offensive coordinator should be simple: find and create the best matchup for his team.

Using Motion and Formation

The possibilities are endless, but the offensive coordinator must know how the defense will align and have built in adjustments in his system to shift and motion into the formations he desires. Once he has this built in, the **concepts** of the offense do not change, just the formations he uses. Simple for the athletes.

"It is impossible to outplay an opponent you cannot outthink".
Lawson Little

CHAPTER 5

THE "BLEND"

The "Blend"

"I need to do a better job of putting my players in a position to make plays."
Andy Reid

It is my belief that Andy Reid is one of the best, most innovative coaches on the offensive side of the ball. From his time with Philadelphia and now in Kansas City, he has always been very creative and successful. If a coach like him can say he "needs to do a better job of putting players in a position to make plays", then we all need to take a look in the mirror. One of the ways he has been so creative is by "blending" RPOs, formation shifts and motions. Watching his offense makes a defensive coordinator's head spin, but the reality is he is dressing up many of the same **concepts**, by tagging an RPO or a route adjustment.

The "Blend" is when an offensive coordinator starts to mix in RPOs, formations, motions and tempo with all of the **concepts** the offense runs. This is a way to put more pressure on the defense if the base offense is not working as well as it should be. Or, it can be a way to create confusion for the defense. Each element on its own is difficult to stop, but when an offense is able to blend all of these together in an organized manner, it is very tough on a defense to get lined up, much less to gameplan to stop the offensive system.

The "Blend"

The beautiful part is that it doesn't change the concept for the offensive players. It simply changes how the offense arrives at the **concept**. Simple for the offense, but much more difficult for the defense. Think about the problems this will present to the defense. They must have the adjustments built in for motion, formations, RPOs and of course attempt to stop the base **concepts** the offense is running. Once the offense has a system with built in motions, shifts, formations and tags, this can be as creative as the offensive coordinator wants to get.

As a younger offensive coach, I'd recommend building up to this point. None of the "extra" matters if the offense cannot run the base **concept** well. Focus on that portion and limit the number of base **concepts** being taught. Once the base **concept** is taught, understood and able to be adjusted, then proceed on to the "blend". It is great to be able to help the offense, but it will not be successful if this is at the start of the offense, not the end.

Becoming great at the fundamentals of the offense should always take precedence before adding the "blend". Spend time in practice on drills that will immediately translate to the field. In my experience, I have seen too much time spent on drills that do not translate to what the offense is attempting to accomplish. The drill may be a great drill, but if the offense is hopeful to put in all the "extras", the team cannot afford to waste time on drills that do not directly correlate to what happens in a game.

The "Blend"

Once a program has established being great at the fundamentals needed to execute their **concepts**, they can begin to become more and more creative in their approach. It is important to focus on the fundamentals needed for the specific **concepts** the offense will run. Too often coaches run drills simply because they have seen them at other established programs, and they do not ask why that drill works for that program.

While there are many "universal" drills that would fit at any program, there are a few drills that will work for your program due to the **concepts** your offense runs. A simple example would be offensive line steps and stance drills will drastically change due to the style of offense and the concepts the offense runs. The same is said for each position on the offense. Simply put, make sure your drills match what you hope to see during a game.

Here are a few areas covered and how they can be blended to become difficult for a defense:

Tempo + Formations
Motion + RPO game
Tempo + Motion

An offense can use these tools and more to put strain on the defense by working the same **concepts**, but gaining an advantage for their players.

The "Blend"

Tempo + Formations

Using tempo is a great way to stress a defense. Using formations is another way to cause issues for a defense. When an offense combines the two, it becomes extremely difficult for a defense to get aligned correctly, much less to execute any stunts or even read their keys correctly. Much of their practice time that week will have to be dedicated to getting ready for multiple looks, and throwing in change in tempo makes that even more difficult to prepare for in a week.

While using fast tempo is the main way most offense accomplish confusing a defense, and that is a great one, it is not the only way that tempo and formations can be combined. Another way many Wing T teams have been using for decades is the quick break from the huddle. An offense huddles close to the football and breaks as quickly as possible before running a play. The defense must find the formation and align correctly in under 5 seconds.

When an offense uses this tactic and throws in exotic or "unbalanced" formations, it can become very difficult for a defense. The offense is running the exact same **concepts** they know and understand, but they are mixing in two weapons to make it much more difficult for the defense. Simple for the offense, but difficult for the defense.

The "Blend"

Motion + RPO game
Another way to make an offense difficult to defend is to mix motions with the RPO game. This is usually best done with a quick motion right before the snap of the ball. There are many ways to do this and cause conflict for a defense.

Here are a couple of examples:

To motion a running back out and tying a screen RPO with a base run. Most offenses have a similar **concept** already built-in to it. If the numbers or leverage favor the screen pre-snap, the quarterback throws the ball, and if the numbers favor the run, he hands it off or runs the ball. Mixing in a quick motion pre-snap is a way to give him a very clean and simple read. If the defense moves out, run the ball. If they do not move, throw the screen.

Another example is to motion a wide receiver across the formation and have him run a chute/bubble route. The quarterback snaps the ball as he is crossing the center and reads his normal progression for a post-snap RPO. There will be an example in the later portion of this book of that exact play. For the defense, it forces them to move coverage all the way across the field, or allow the offense to gain leverage with the pass.

The "Blend"

Tempo + Motion
Using tempo or motion alone is difficult for a defense to prepare for, but when they are combined it becomes even more difficult. When an offense has the ability to change the speed of the tempo, especially to a faster tempo, it causes a level of stress on a defense. Offenses that also make use of motioning across the formation from the backfield, or into the backfield also cause a strain on the defense. However, when "blended" together they can become a very big problem for the defense.

There are multiple ways an offensive coordinator can use these two tools with his **concepts**. Here are a couple of simple examples:

By aligning in a trips look or empty look an offensive coordinator will usually get a "check" that the defense has shown on film. This is especially true if the offense is running up-tempo. The offense then can motion/shift a player across the formation or from the backfield to create a numbers advantage or a personnel advantage as the defense must quickly shift to answer the change in formation.

Lining up in a look and shifting multiple players at one time is difficult for a defense. If an offense can quickly shift the strength of the formation and snap the ball in under five seconds the defense will be forced to make a very difficult decision. Do they attempt to bring the personnel with the shift, or do they simply bump over?

The "Blend"

In the following pages we will again look at the "Blend" using Buck Sweep as our **concept**. Dressing up a **concept** with a mixture of formations, motions, RPO game to make a simple **concept** appear to be complicated for the defense is the key in all offenses. Whether or not you run Buck, this line of thinking is key for all offensive systems.

In this section you will see motions/shifts to create a numbers advantage or create a conflict player. Motion can also assist the offense by causing the defense to shift late, creating an advantage.

The RPO game does not change, but with formation manipulation and motions, the offense can create a much cleaner "conflict defender".

The "Blend"

Red-Empty-Fly-Buck-Peak

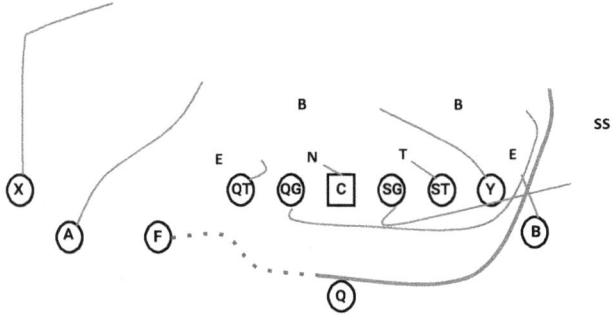

This is a very simple way to run the same **concept**, but to align in empty to create a lighter box. Nothing changes for the offense except for a slow motion from an empty set.

Red-Empty-Q Buck-Fast

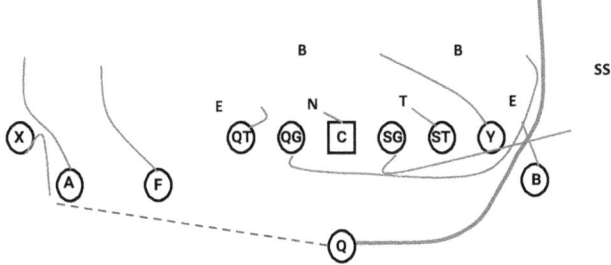

If a team is wanting to run the QB, this is another simple way to create a light box or an easy screen. Pre-snap is a numbers game on the screen or the run.

The "Blend"

Trips Left - Q Buck-Fast

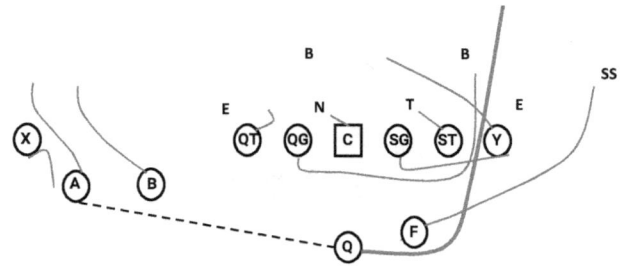

Another simple way to create a strain on the defense is a quick pre-snap read for the QB/Coach. If the defense puts numbers to the screen, run the ball.

Red-Over-Train-Buck

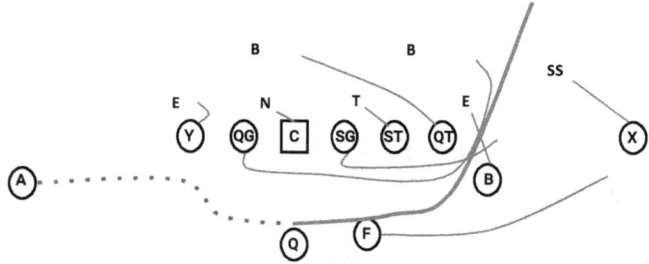

This is not an RPO, but a way to add an additional blocker by running the same run **concept** out of an unbalanced look.

The "Blend"

Blue-Buck-Bubble-Go

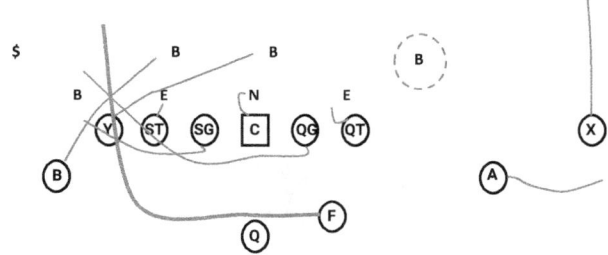

This is a more "expensive" RPO as it gives the QB a few options. It is a way to put a strain on the corner as well as the force player.

Blue-Motion-Q-Buck

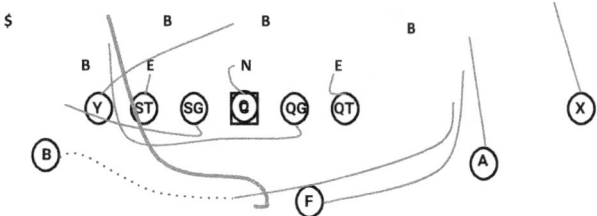

This is the same run **concept**, but with some misdirection from a motion. This could become a read if the QB was able to read the backside LB or DE. Or, it could simply be window dressing.

The "Blend"

Buck-Glance

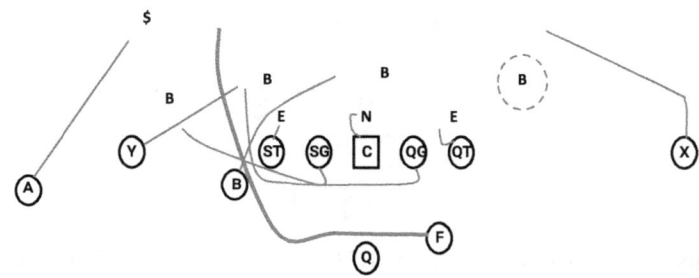

The "Blend" of buck can be almost endless. Using formation, motions and RPOs make an old play almost a new concept. Once an offensive coordinator understands how a defense is reacting to formations and motions, building in RPOs is almost easy. Working to isolate defensive players that are identified as conflict players is a great way to make the offense click. By using motion and formations the offense can cause different defenders to become the "conflict defender" and then RPO off of them.

The "Blend"

The "Blend" is how offense can separate themselves. While I have already cautioned about doing too much, I live by a quote I heard from an old coach one day:

*"Plays (**concepts**) are expensive, but formations are cheap".*

If installed correctly, using multiple formations, shifts and motions should come down to the ability of the coach. As coaches become more and more comfortable in their own system, they are able to add more of the "Blend" and make what is simple for their athletes appear complex for a defense.

The rest of this book will be using multiple examples to illustrate how to apply some of these principles in your offense. Please do not become so focused on these exact **concepts**, that you feel those are the primary point of the book. Instead, simply see them as an example to what a coach can do to dress up his **concepts**. While I am using examples that I have more experience with, these principles apply to any offense.

"You have all the tools and resources you need. What you do with them is up to you".
Cherie Carter-Scott

CHAPTER 6

COMMON MISTAKES

Common Mistakes

When learning to call offenses there are some very common mistakes many make. I know from experience on many of the points discussed in this chapter that there are plenty of ways to create issues in an offense. This chapter will discuss some of the more common mistakes made when installing an offensive system.

Common Mistakes

1) Doing too much

1) Not having built-in adjustments

1) Giving up too quickly on a **concept**

1) Not running **concepts** that match your team

Each of these mistakes are common issues with many offensive coordinators, myself included. Most coaches understand these on the front end, but get caught up with the excitement of the season, or they get discouraged by how long the process may take.

Common Mistakes

Doing too much

"Too often people get stuck in a state of over-thinking. The result is that they never make a decision."
Steve Backley

This is very common with many coaches working at the high school or lower levels in football. While it is great to have many potential answers, usually the team that runs their own **concepts** best, wins. Many offenses have a huge variety of plays, but do not have **concepts** that are adjustable to work against any defense. Thus, they often are forced to abandon plays and add more into their playbook.

My second season as a head coach, I called the offense. When we played a veteran coach that I felt had a similar talent set, we got smoked. It was embarrassing for me to see how rough our offense looked. Not one play seemed to look sharp. I tried about 20-30 plays that game with little to no success.

After the game was over, I called the coach and spoke with him at length. He was very polite, but honest in letting me know that we had too much in and were never going to be great at any of the plays if we had to work on them all. That weekend we scratched about half our plays, started working to become experts at those we had, then working to create adjustments, reads and formations. In short, we moved to a **concept-based** offense in week two.

Common Mistakes

That season we would go on to win the conference and have (at that point) one of the most explosive offenses that school had seen. We secured our first home-playoff game in over 20 years. While there were plenty of other factors, by simplifying our offense and becoming **concept-based**, we became more potent than ever before.

Our practices were smoother and shorter and our players had much more confidence in what we were trying to accomplish. While we were able to add formations, motions and other options as the season progressed, we never lost sight of being a **concept-based** team. It was a great lesson that I was taught, but must continually remind myself of as a coach.

It is important as a coach that we do not lose sight of the fact that fundamentals are more important than schemes. Teaching a **concept** is very important, but we need to be sure to teach what makes it successful. Do not put the cart before the horse, and have great schemes and formations and shifts, but lose out on time to teach how to make it successful.

Common Mistakes

Not having built in adjustments

"Great acts are made up of small deeds."
Lao Tzu

Think about practice and how many times the offensive coordinator will get frustrated with the scout defense because they are not "lining up right". I know personally, I have about lost it in this situation. However, the reality is we have no idea what we will see on defense. Those guys get paid to make adjustments and to stop the offense.

A huge mistake in many offenses is to move so quickly past a play that they have set up perfectly if the defense would only cooperate and do what they anticipate. But that play will not work if it is a different look. Teaching rules-based **concepts** should eliminate this issue, but too often we want to put in as many "plays" to take advantage of an anticipated look that we don't simply take what is already installed in the offense and tweak it. Instead of fixing what is wrong, we want to think the entire **concept** is flawed. Often, we simply have not put enough time and effort into making sure we have thought through all the "If-Then" situations.

Common Mistakes

When facing a defense, the **concept** should already have built-in adjustments. While adjusting a formation, motion, RPO or influence block is a great thing to add, putting in a completely different play usually never works.

Instead put the time into becoming an expert at the **concept** and ways in which to protect it with adjustments.

Teach the athletes the "why" behind the **concept** as well. They will then be able to understand potential adjustments that need to be made. When a team reaches the point that the players understand the adjustments needed, they have a great chance to be successful.

Common Mistakes

Giving up on a concept too quickly

"Get the fundamentals down and the level of everything you do will rise."
Michael Jordan

In the middle of a game, offensive play callers (myself included) are quick to associate a negative play with a bad **concept**. It is natural that if you call it in a game and it does not work, it must be a bad **concept**. There have been many games that I have gone back and watched a game only to recognize that we were one blown assignment away from a very explosive play.

Often, the easy move is to simply move away from a **concept** because it was not executed. Or, it may need to have some small adjustments. Once a team has committed to a **concept**, it needs to continually be refined and tweaked, but should never be abandoned.

When my offenses have struggled, it is usually the first thought to get out of a **concept**, since it is the easier move. While that may need to happen, it should be done only after research on why the **concept** is struggling. Usually, after some research, there are a few problems that can be solved to fix the issue. If it is a **concept** that does not match our team, we may look at taking it off the table, but again, this is only after exhausting other possibilities.

Common Mistakes

Not running concepts that match your team

"The art of being wise is knowing what to overlook."
William James

There are a multitude of very successful football teams. Many of them run very different offensive systems with completely different **concepts**. Yet, all are successful with what they do. Deciding on what system or **concepts** to run should always boil down to one question:

Does this fit our athletes?

When I moved from Montgomery, Alabama to Southside Batesville, Arkansas, it was a very different shift as far as the abilities of our athletes. While it was possible to be successful at both places, it was not wise to run the same style of offense. Unfortunately for me, it took a little time to realize this. While I loved the spread and throwing the ball, that was not the wisest move for our athletes. The **concepts** were sound, but they did not fit our athletes.

It took a big adjustment from me as the coach to become uncomfortable and look at other schemes and **concepts** that fit our talent level compared to our opponents. Once we found what matched our athletes, for us it was the buck sweep and gap scheme, it was amazing how much better our team looked.

CHAPTER 7

RUN GAME SECTION

-BUCK
-ISO
-COUNTER

Overview

The entire goal of this book is to show how to take one **concept** and install everything needed to keep and allow the **concept** to be successful against all fronts that a team will see. In this section I have chosen three base plays:

Buck Sweep
Iso
Counter

I am showing these from my base formation, but each can be run from multiple formations and looks. After the base play is shown, then the section will give the following:

Base rules

Play against multiple fronts

Formations that can help create match-ups for an offense

Motions that can create problems for a defense

Blocking tags that can help with potential problems

RPO game that attaches to the play

The "Blend" – examples of putting it all together

Overview

When **concepts** are taught and players understand what the goal of each **concept** is, then adjustments are simple and easy. Then **concepts** can be built upon by adding motion, RPO game and other movements. Use this section as more of an example. While I hope to give some insight on those specific plays, the larger picture is how to install **concepts** for your offense.

BUCK SWEEP

Buck

Buck sweep or "pin and pull" is a **concept** several teams have gone to recently from the shotgun. In this section I will attempt to walk through how teaching Buck as a **concept** allows for the play to become multiple.

Realize that the same teaching of **concepts** could apply to outside zone or other outside run schemes. I am simply using Buck as an example for this book. Take the thought process and apply it to whatever outside run your offensive system will highlight.

When teaching a **concept**, we will go through the same process as the beginning of the book. In this section you will find:

Base rules

Blocking vs. all fronts – Teaching how to make quick adjustments

Using formations and motions – Think like a Defensive Coordinator

RPO's that can be attached to Buck

The "Blend" – using motions, formations and RPO game to make the play difficult to stop and give answers to all defenses.

Buck

While much of this is in earlier chapters of the book, I wanted to include this entire section laid out together to help with the process of how a **concept** will come together.   This thought process works for any **concept**, but I have a special place in my heart for Buck Sweep and wanted to show a few examples of how to make it potent.

Buck Sweep

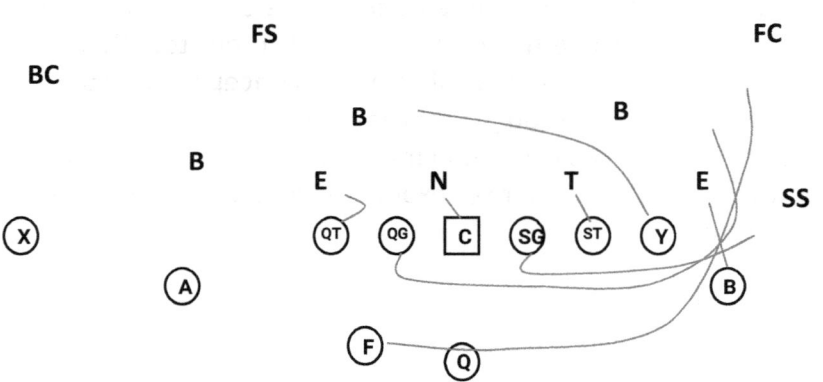

Position	Assignment
X	RPO Called – Later in Chapter
A	RPO Called – Later in Chapter
F	Cross QB Face – Stay Horizontal 3 Steps – Follow Guard
Y	Gap-Down-Backer
B	Gap-Down-Backer
QT	Gap-Hinge – Unless RPO Tag is Used
QG	Pull Wrap
C	On-Backside
SG	Pull Kick
ST	Gap-Down-Backer
Q	

Buck
Blocking Rules Vs. Fronts

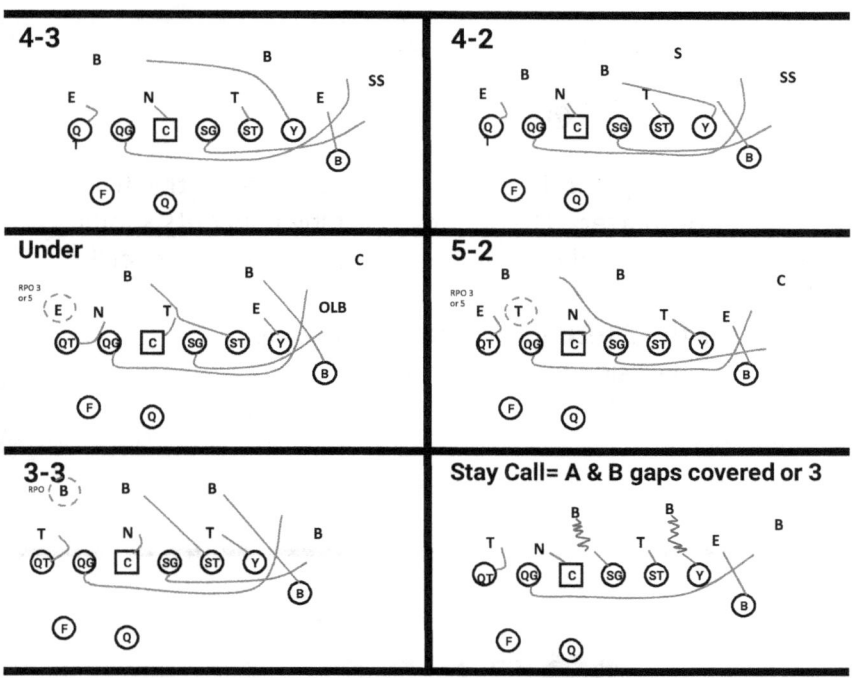

These are just a few examples of the fronts a run must be prepared to face. When teaching concepts, most teams will be "rules-based". For Buck Sweep the rule is "gap-down-backer" on the play side.

This allows for the linemen to simply follow their rules, and they should be able to pick up any front that the defense will show. It may not be the optimal way to block the front, but the rules make is simple and clear.

Buck
Blocking Rules Vs. Fronts

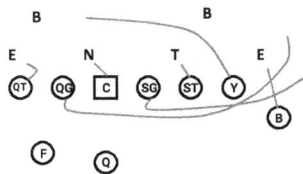

When teaching the base rules of buck sweep, the front should not matter. That is why teaching **concepts** should allow for an easily adjustable front. For this specific front:
Wing has the 9 technique – he is "in his gap"
Y has the backside LB – he is "backer"
Tackle has the 3 technique – he is "in his gap"
Guards pull
Backside Tackle will step-hinge

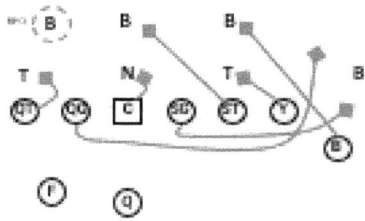

Again, teaching **concepts** should allow any front to be accounted for. In this front:
Wing blocks LB – his rule is "gap-down-backer", since no defensive lineman is in his gap or down, he has LB
Y – blocks "down"
Tackle – blocks "backer"
Guards pull
Backside Tackle will step-hinge
In this front – the backside linebacker is unaccounted for, so the QB must read him

Buck
Using Formations and Motions

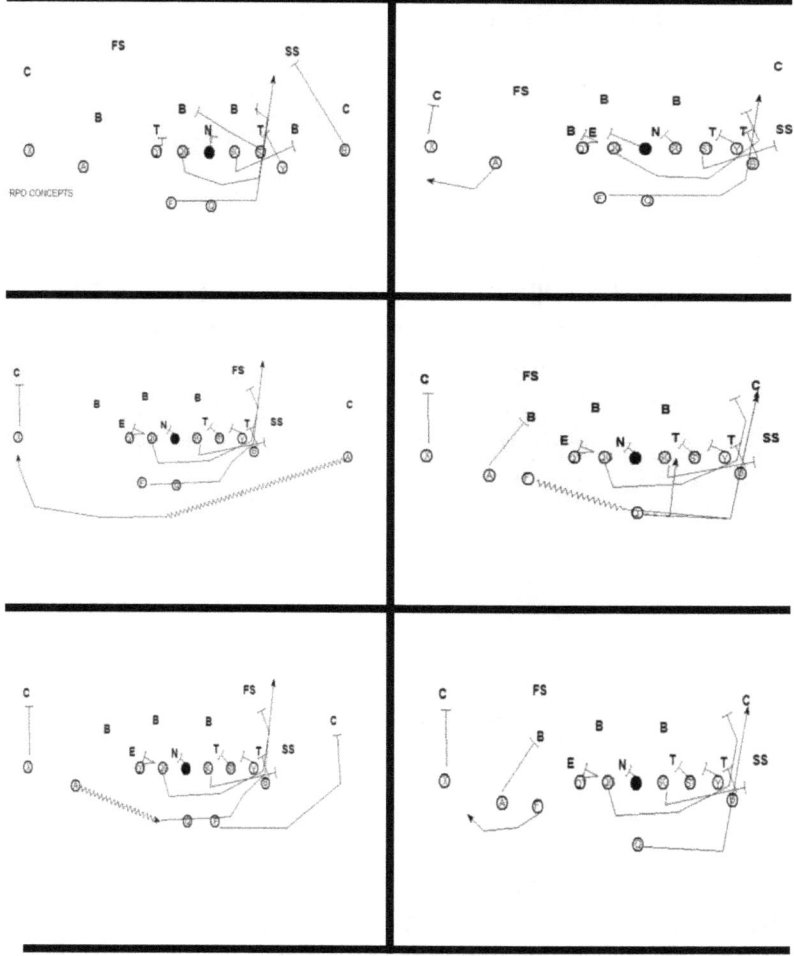

These are just a few examples using formations and motion to manipulate the defense into aligning how the offense wants them to. Using formations and then motions can create problems if used correctly.

Buck
Using Formations and Motions

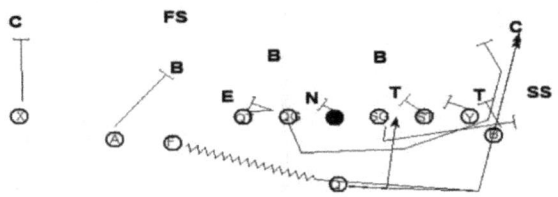

In the first example the offense aligns in an Empty set. Generally, this will cause the defense to get into a 2-high look or lighten the box. The offense then simply brings the same player in motion to run buck sweep. It changes nothing for any player, other than the motion, but to a defense it causes a lighter box and a quick adjusting safety or DB.

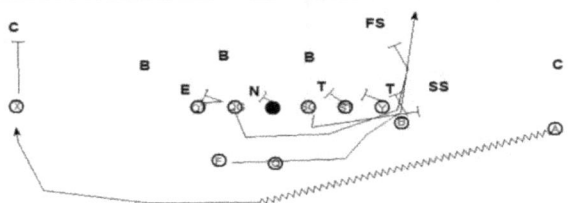

In this example the offense lines up in a Trips-Strong look. The use of motion (designed for a man-to-man team) will cause the defense problems as they have to either run with the motion, or roll the secondary.

In both plays the offense simply motioned players to create a problem for the defense and used formations to get the alignment they wanted.

Buck
Play Side Blocking Tags

"Bypass"
Tells B to "bypass" the 9 Technique
Strong Guard will kick out on 9 Technique

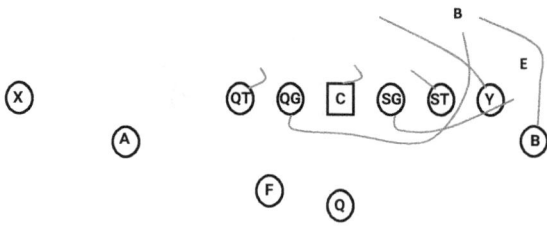

"Dubs"
Tells Y and B to double team
Y vertical push
B horizontal push
Work to backside backer

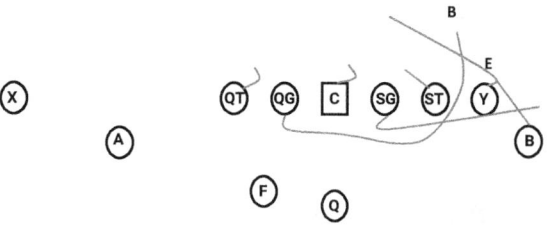

Buck
Play Side Blocking Tags

"Stay"
A and B gaps covered or threatened
C and SG block Down
QG has kick out

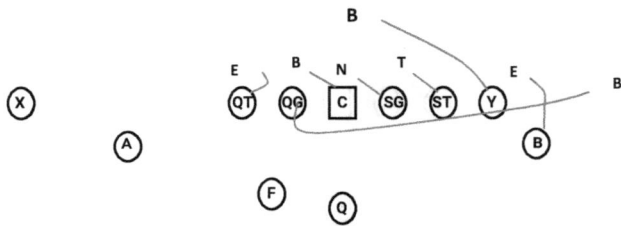

Teaching "tags" to the base concept has been good to us. Once the players understand the base concept, we start to introduce adjustments that only "speak" to 1-2 players. We use the term "tag" and use these often, since we run our concepts often instead of adding multiple plays.

On this page our "Buck-Stay" would often be referred to as more of a "Trap" play. But, by keeping the terminology simple it is easier for our athletes to understand what we are teaching.

On the previous page we simply built in some tags to help with potential problems – a dominant defensive end.

Buck
RPO Tags

"Peak"
A Works inside leverage, X a Post. QB Reads ILB

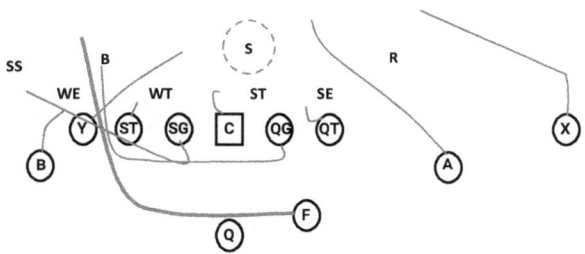

"Key"
Can throw fast screen (A steps on toes of "X" and blocks Most Dangerous). Post snap QB reads ILB for a run

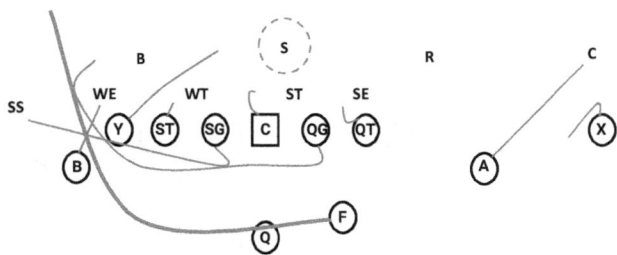

Buck
RPO Tags

"Read and Bogo"
QB reads the 5 tech. Can throw bubble post snap

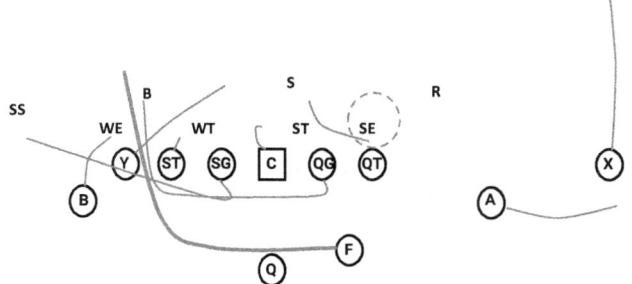

"Steal"
QB reads the 4i/3 tech

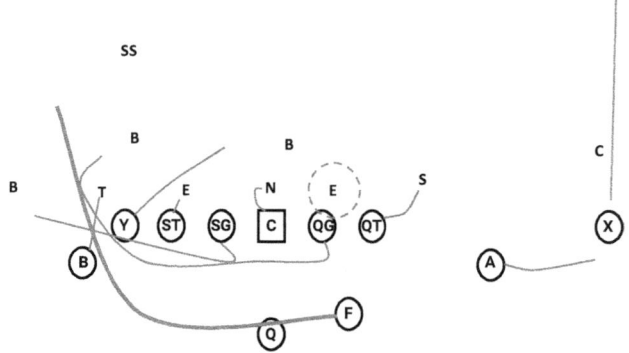

Buck
RPO Tags

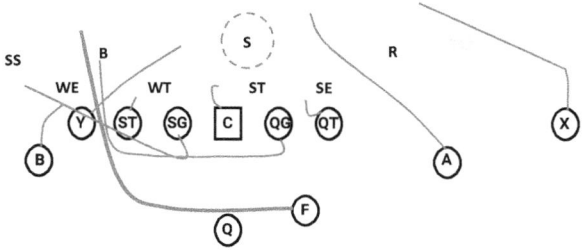

RPOs can be as exotic as a coach wants to make them. Here is a simple one that many teams run. The QB would read the backside linebacker and throw the "peak" or "spot" route behind him if he commits to the run. If he sits, then hand the ball off to the RB.

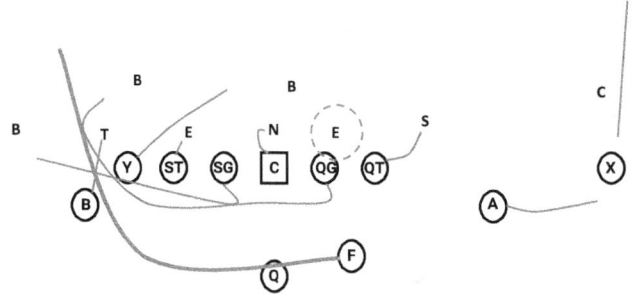

In this RPO, the tag "steal" tells the right tackle to block out to the OLB and leave the DE alone. The QB reads the DE, and if he crashes he pulls the ball. We have tagged this with a bubble and a go and the next read becomes the corner on the bubble or go route. This could also be tagged with a fast screen or simple bubble route if needed.

Buck
The "Blend"

Red-Empty-Fly-Buck-Peak

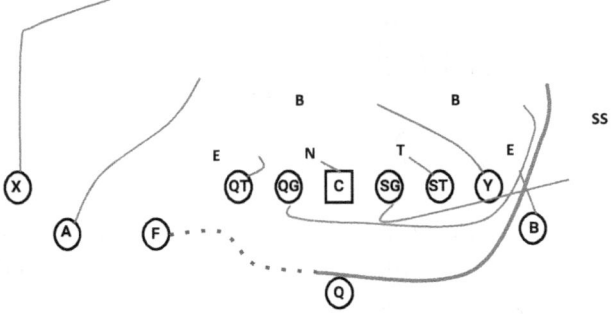

This is a very simple way to run the same **concept**, but to align in empty to create a lighter box. Nothing changes for the offense except for a slow motion from an empty set.

Red-Empty-Q Buck-Fast

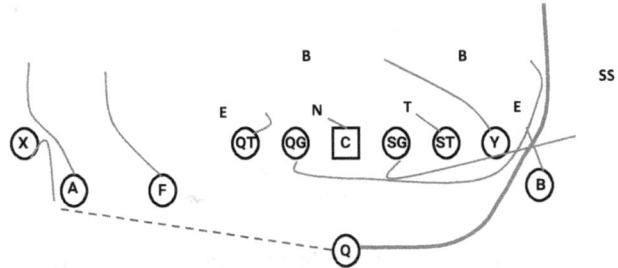

If a team is wanting to run the QB, this is another simple way to create a light box or an easy screen. Pre-snap is a numbers game on the screen or the run.

Buck
The "Blend"

Trips Left - Q Buck-Fast

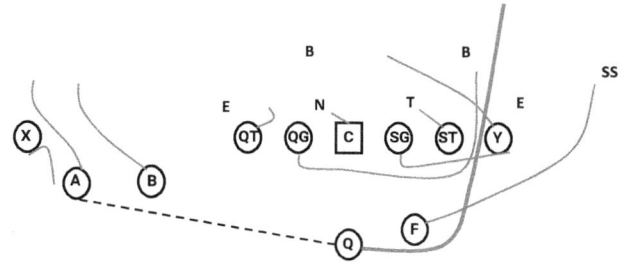

This is another simple way to create a strain on the defense. This is a quick pre-snap read for the QB/Coach. If the defense puts numbers to the screen, run the ball.

Red-Over-Train-Buck

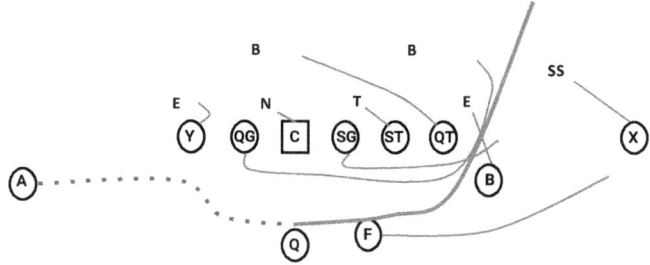

This is not an RPO, but a way to add an additional blocker is by running the same run **concept** out of an unbalanced look.

Buck
The "Blend"

Buck-Glance

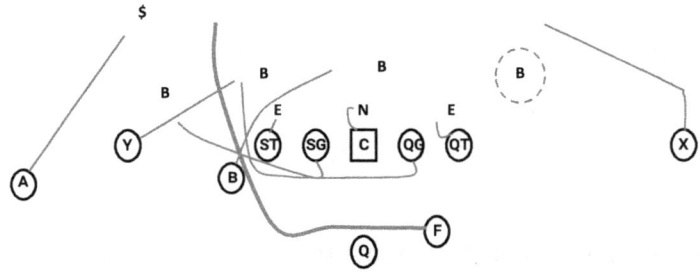

The "Blend" of Buck can be almost endless. Using formation, motions and RPOs make an old play almost a new concept. Once an offensive coordinator understands how a defense is reacting to formations and motions, building in RPOs is almost easy. Working to isolate defensive players that are identified as conflict players is a great way to make the offense click. By using motion and formations, the offense can cause different defenders to become the "conflict defender" and then RPO off of them.

Buck
If-Then

IF the defense overloads to stop Buck Sweep

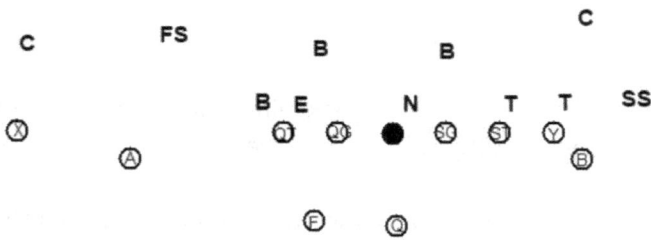

THEN

1) ISO – Block out on Defensive line and run underneath SS

1) Strong side play action – Read the corner for the shot play

1) B-Pop or X Crack and go – If corner is very aggressive make the read simple for your QB

1) Waggle – More than likely TE will come wide open in this look

1) RPO Game on the backside – Steal would be a good call here for QB pull. Could also just throw quick game depending on depth of DB's

1) Counter – Counter is also an option in this look

Buck
If-Then

IF we are not able to get movement against a 9 Technique

THEN

1) Run "bypass" and kick him out if he is an up-field penetrating defensive player

1) Have the TE base him for 1-count before releasing inside on buck sweep

1) Widen his splits by alignment

1) Run "trade" and move your TE/Wing away from him pre-snap

As you work through the Buck Sweep more in depth, you will find other issues that must be addressed. This book is not meant to be an in-depth study of Buck Sweep, but simply showing how each part of the **concept** must be planned for and taught to the athletes.

If you would like more depth on the Buck Sweep there are multiple materials available at FBCoachsimpson.com.

ISOLATION

ISO

Each offensive system will have their own way to teach the ISO **concept**. In this book, I will share how we teach the play, but do not let that become the focal point of the chapter. Instead, I am hoping that this play can simply serve as another example to **conceptual** teaching.

When we install this **concept**, here is how we teach it with our offensive line:

Backside Tackle – Gap-Hinge (he also is the RPO tag)
Backside Guard – Pull Wrap – First Daylight
Center – On-Backside.
Play side Guard - #1 Defensive Lineman
Play side Tackle - #2 Defensive Lineman, unless #2 is outside "C gap"
Play side Tight End – Block Out

Once we teach our linemen the rules, they can handle any front the defense may throw against them. In the following pages are several examples, but it is our hope that no matter what front they may see, their rules should take care of the blocking.

We teach our skill players the base rules of the run, but also pair this with our RPO screen and passing game. Often, they will not be involved with the run, but we want them to be aware of what is happening.

ISO

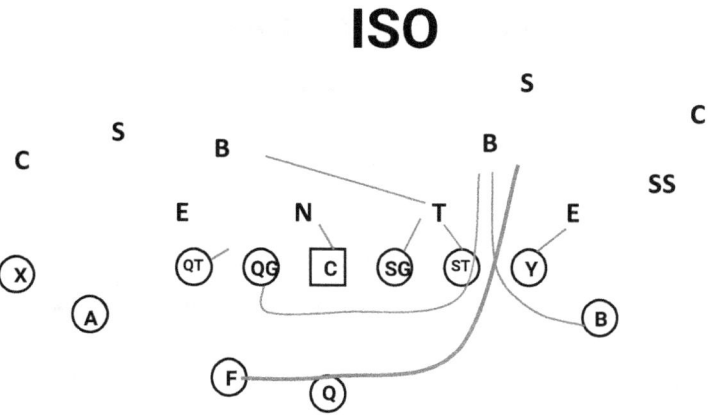

Position	Assignment
X	RPO or Pass Concept
A	RPO or Pass Concept
F	Step to the QB, then downhill, following the guard insert
Y	Block out
B	Insert in first available gap
QT	Gap-Hinge – OR RPO CONCEPT
QG	Skip Pull to first available gap
C	On - Backside
SG	Block #1 defensive lineman to backside backer
ST	Block #2 defensive lineman…unless #2 is outside the Y
Q	RPO Read

ISO
Blocking Rules Vs. Fronts

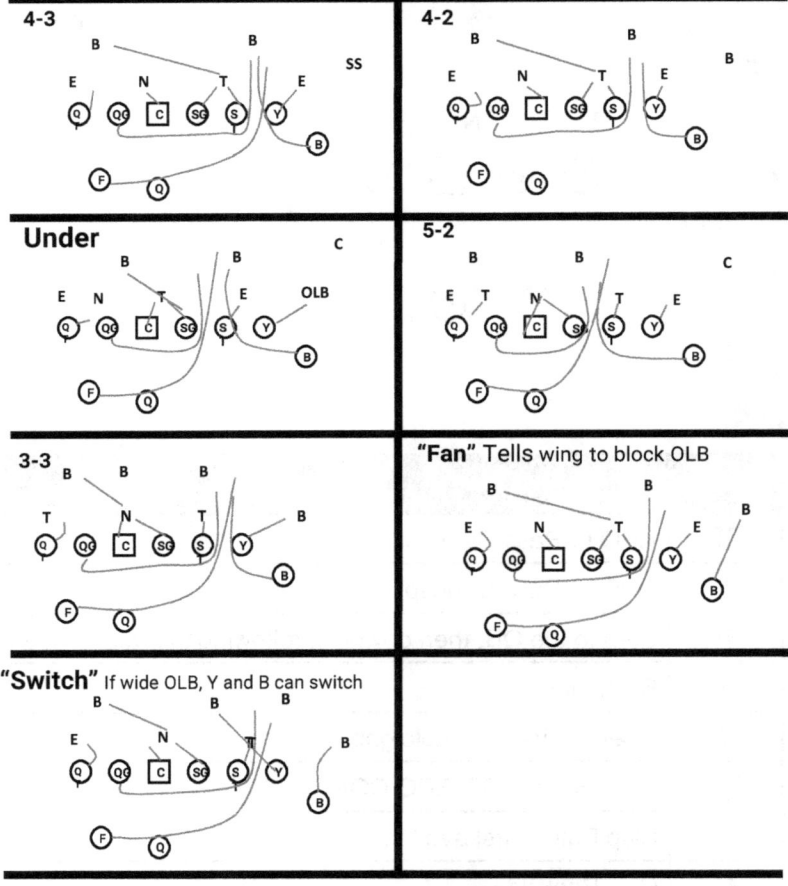

Many will refer to this play as power/gut or another name. Either way, the point of the section is to show how once rules are taught, the offensive line should be able to adjust to all fronts. Teaching the **concept** of the play allows for adjustments to be made.

ISO
Blocking Rules Vs. Fronts

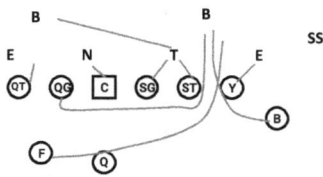

When teaching a rules-based **concept**, it should naturally answer all questions to different fronts. Reviewing the rules:

Y – blocks out on the 9 technique
Tackle – blocks #1 DL (since #2 is outside the Y)
Guard – blocks #1 DL (this is the double team)
Center – blocks on-backside
Backside Guard/B – insert easiest path
Backside Tackle – Step-Hinge

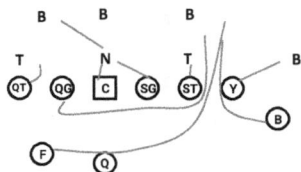

Here is the same concept against a 3-3 stack team.

Y – blocks out on the OLB
Tackle – blocks #2 DL
Guard – blocks #1 DL (this is double team)
Center – blocks on-backside
Backside Guard/B – insert easiest path
Backside Tackle – Step-Hinge
*Against a 3-3 the QB must read one LB's with an RPO

ISO
Using Formations and Motions

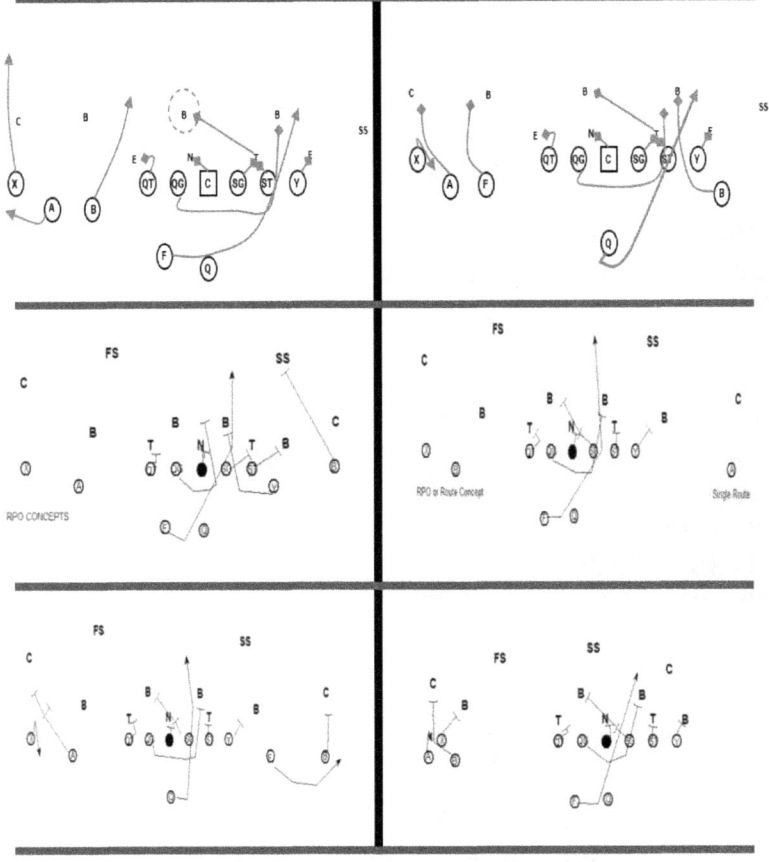

Formations to create a numbers advantage cause a defense to indicate their intent. These are just a few formations that can be used to run ISO. Each poses different issues to the defense and allows for different RPO concepts.

ISO
Using Formations and Motions

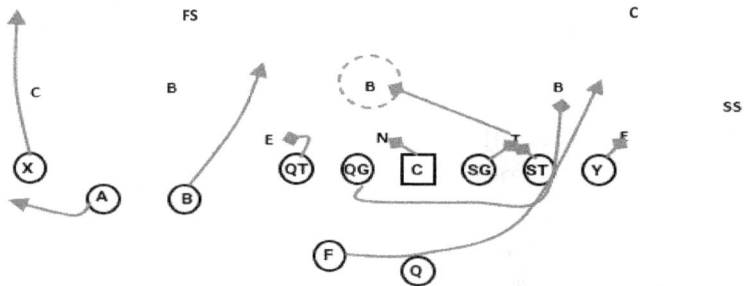

In the first example the offense has lined up in a trips look to lighten the box of the defense and isolate that backside linebacker for the "peak" RPO **concept**. By going trips the offense has created space and forced the linebacker to become the "conflict" player.

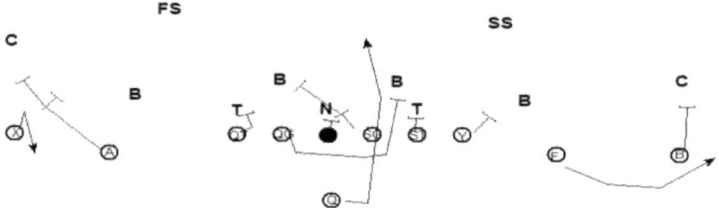

This example has spread the defense wide and created a lot of horizontal space. Most defenses will react to an empty set by going into a two-high look. The formation creates strain on the defense to honor the wide receivers as well as react to a six-man surface at the line. This can be "dressed" up even more by motioning a wide receiver pre-snap or from the backfield.

ISO
RPOs to tag with ISO

This section will include RPOs that can be tagged with ISO. What will become obvious very quickly, is that many of these RPOs were also run with Buck Sweep. That is the goal of most offenses and one way that an offense can become very multiple and save time. Using the same RPO terms from one run and applying them to another makes the installation move much quicker since the **concept** of the RPO is already known by the team.

This is also not an exhaustive list of RPOs that can be attached to the play. It is simply a guide to give ideas for coaches as they work to build their own system. Remember from the chapter on RPOs that they can be attached to almost any defender if the team can learn the **concept** and tag associated with the RPO.

ISO
RPOs to tag with ISO

"Peak"
A works inside leverage, X a Post. QB Reads ILB

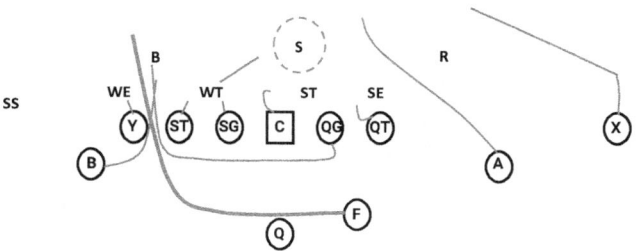

Same read for the QB as he would have on "buck-peak".

"Key"
Can throw fast screen (A steps on toes of "X" and blocks Most Dangerous). Post snap QB reads ILB for a run

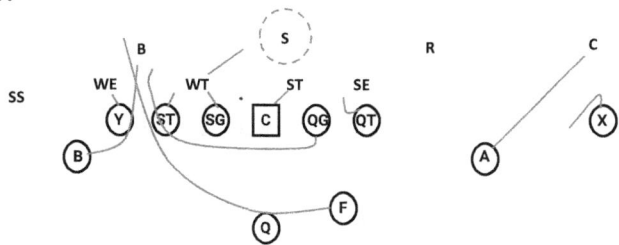

Same read for the QB as he would have on "buck-peak".

ISO
RPOs to tag with ISO

"Read and Bogo"
QB reads the 5 tech. Can throw bubble post snap.

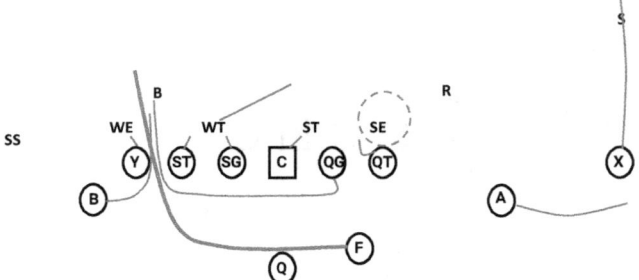

Same read for the QB as he would have on "buck-peak".

"Steal"
QB reads the 4i/3 tech

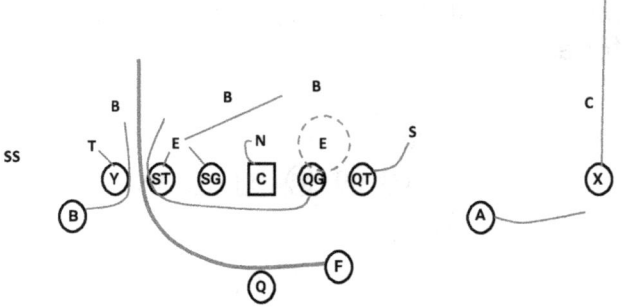

Same read for the QB as he would have on "buck-peak".

ISO
RPOs to tag with ISO

"QB ISO - READ"
QB reads the Defensive End. Can throw screen pre-snap.

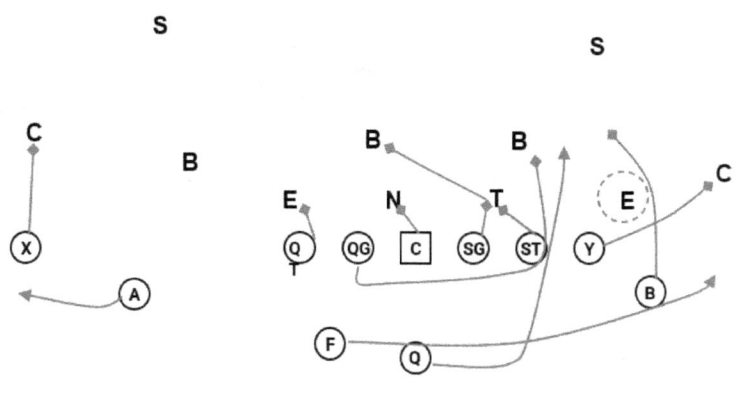

Although in this book this is called ISO, many will call it their flavor of Power/Gut or whatever their name may be for it. The point of the chapter should remain the same. Working to ensure that the rules of the **concept** work against all fronts.

Most would call this play power-read. However, with a simple adjustment the ISO can become this. While this may be more of a time investment, it is simple if the offense is teaching with **concepts**, not simply plays. There is no easier way to install something "new" than to begin the install with the statement, "This is just like ____ with one-two adjustments". That is the goal of teaching **conceptual** football and not simply plays.

ISO
The "Blend"

Red-Flop-ISO-Peak

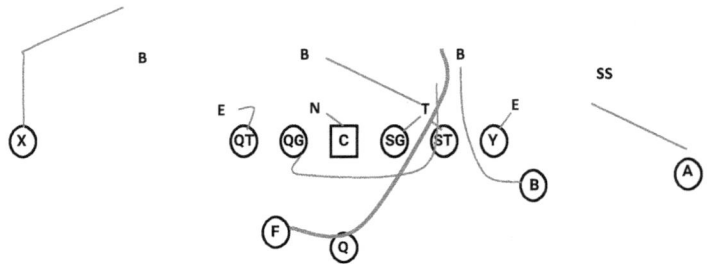

The idea behind the "Blend" is to take the same **concept** and make it difficult on the defense through formations or motions. This is an example of running the exact same "peak" look, but isolating the #1 WR instead of running it to a twins look.

ISO
The "Blend"

Red-Trips-ISO-B-Peak
Q reads ILB

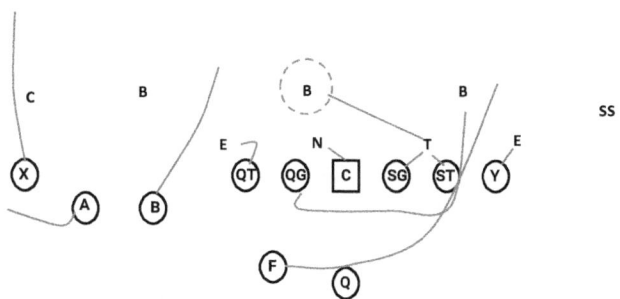

Still the Peak RPO, however the offense is isolating the inside linebacker and reading him. For the QB this is a simple adjustment.

Red-Empty-Q ISO-Now
QB Reads #'s to trips side. A blocks most dangerous. F blocks number 2.

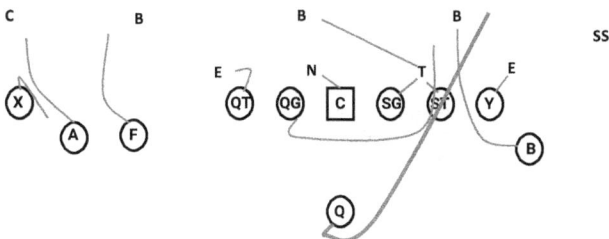

This is the same run, but with the QB out of an empty look. The read is a pre-snap look at numbers.

ISO
The "Blend"

Blue-Motion Tag-ISO
Q fake to B, hand to F

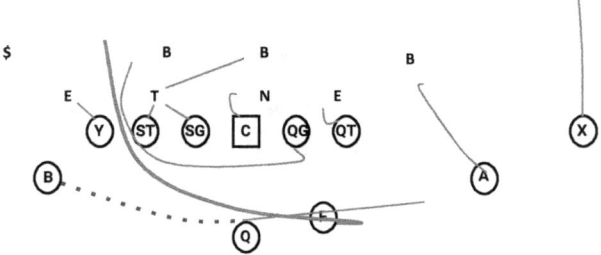

This can be an RPO if the QB could read the OLB or DE – It would just take a simple tag added.

Blue-Flop-Train-ISO-Read-Bubble
Q read first outside the QT. QT scoop second level inside. X block most dangerous.

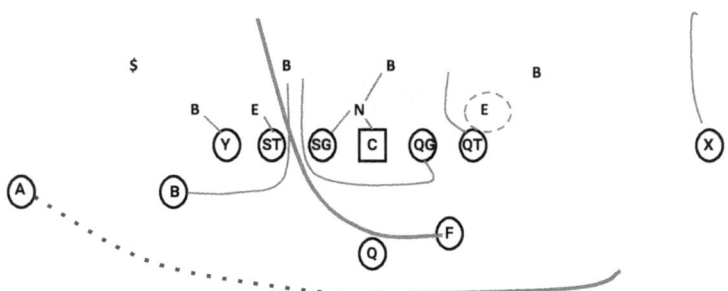

This is the same read for the QB. The only change is the motion from the opposite side of the field.

ISO
If-Then

IF the defense is an up-field penetrating defense:

THEN

1) Widen splits with the Offensive Line and allow penetration as long as it is not condensing the hole

1) Work to create double teams at the point of attack on problem defensive linemen

1) Release backside tackle to the second level defender as the defensive lineman is not squeezing

Defensive fronts are either a "penetrating" front or a "squeezing" front. Both can present problems. We prefer ISO against the fronts that penetrate and Buck against the fronts that are more of a squeezing front. By widening splits an offensive line can help create space for the ISO blocking.

If you would like more depth on the ISO there are multiple materials available at FBCoachsimpson.com.

ISO

ISO, or blast/power, is a common **concept** in most playbooks. The ability to dress it up through formation, shifts, motions, RPOs and tags is what makes it dangerous. It is a simple blocking scheme and a relatively quick install.

When following many of the theories of this book, it can become dangerous. Making a play adjustable to multiple fronts, with multiple RPO **concepts** out of multiple formations, is the entire goal of most offensive systems.

COUNTER

Counter

Counter can be run a few different ways. The old school Wing T approach is to pull the tight end. The easy adjustment for teams running a 20 personnel grouping would be to use the "H" back in that role. Do not let that be the focal point in this section. Instead, focus on the general **concept** and how the adjustments are made.

As with Buck and ISO, Counter is a **concept** that can become as versatile as the imagination. In this section there are a few examples of ways to make counter work, but this is not an all-encompassing work. Most offenses run a flavor of counter, this section will provide some examples of how to make that one play become many.

As with all **concepts** in this book, it is fluid. The rules remain the same for those involved, but the "tags" are endless and make this much more difficult to defend than a traditional counter play.

Counter

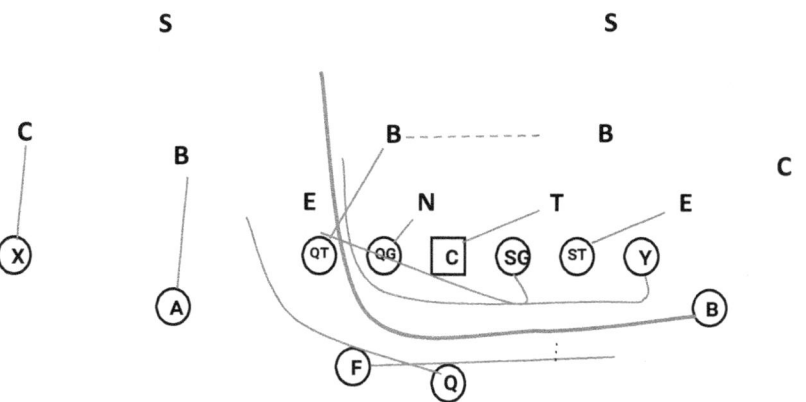

Position	Assignment
X	RPO Concept or Block
A	RPO Concept or Block
F	Take ball from QB and hand underneath to the B
Y	Pull and wrap – first daylight
B	Counter step and take the hand off – follow the Y
QT	Gap – Down - Backer
QG	Gap – Down - Backer
C	Gap – Down - Backer
SG	Pull - Kick
ST	Gap - Hinge
Q	RPO – Or hand off and lead block

Counter
Blocking Rules Vs. Fronts

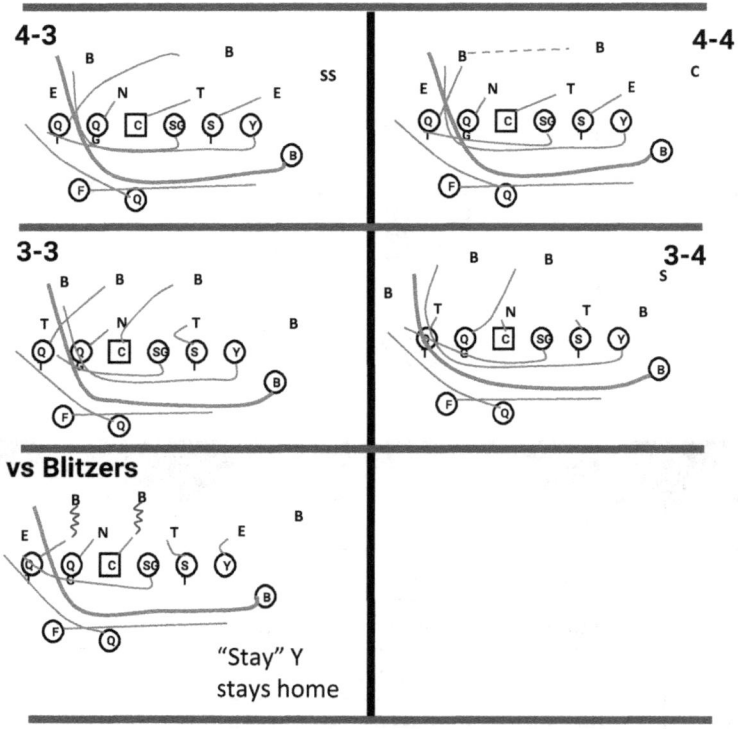

This is the base way we would run counter against the different types of fronts. The play is very straight-forward. Block down on play side, pull-kick with the guard and wrap with the tight end.

When we teach this **concept**, we teach the double hand-off as the base. Later in this section, we will show the different ways we dress up this **concept** to help our offense.

Counter
Play Side Blocking Tags

"LOCK"
QT blocks out on DE

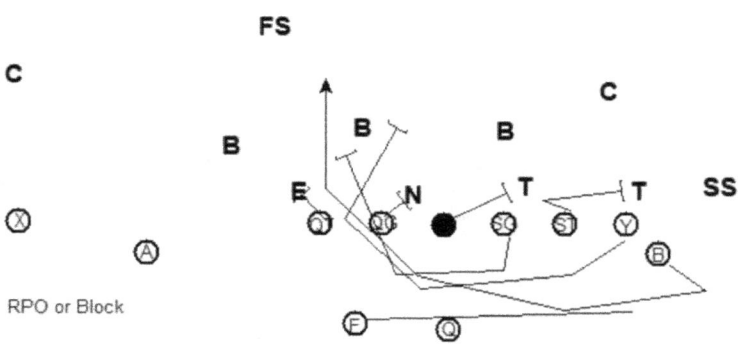

Lock talks to our Backside Tackle on Counter. This allows him to "base out" the 5 technique instead of following his general rules to down block.

We love this look against teams that have a very hard squeezing Defensive End or against teams we can manipulate with our splits.

The adjustment for the pulling Guard is now to wrap into B-Gap instead of pulling and kicking.

Counter
Play Side Blocking Tags

"STAY"
Y does not pull – Must Crack with WR's

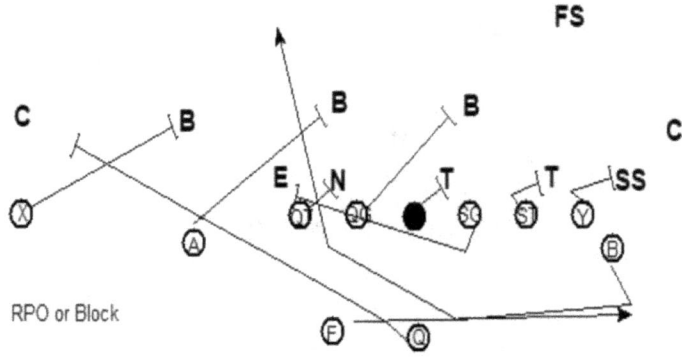

A "stay" call speaks to our Y. He now understands not to pull.

Usually this is done if a team has a very well coached Defensive End or Outside Linebacker that would chase down the counter.

If this is called, the offense must understand that an inside linebacker will not be accounted for in the blocking scheme. He must either be blocked through misdirection, or with a skill player.

Counter
Play Side Blocking Tags

"Switch"
G and T switch roles

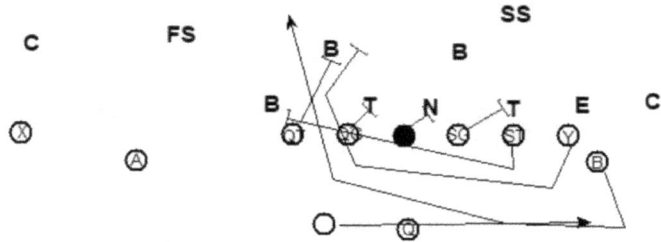

Switch speaks to our pullers. This is a way of literally switching responsibilities. The lineman responsible for pulling now will gap-protect and the next lineman over will pull.

In this example, we have switched our Guard and Tackle on the right side. The Guard will not gap-protect and the Tackle will pull and kick.

Having this available for us helps against "bear" fronts or against teams that like to stunt.

Counter
Play Side Blocking Tags

"Keep"
F keeps the ball – vs. chasing defense

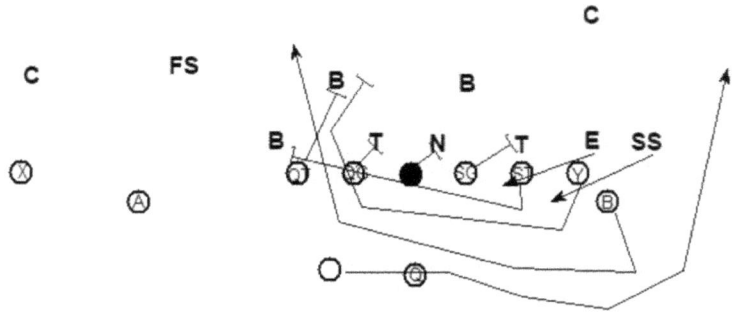

"Keep" is a call made by the coach when the defense is over playing the counter. While it can be an RPO if run by the QB, in this example it is a designed call.

This call came about while using the "IF-THEN" chart.

IF – The defense is crashing hard to chase down counter.

THEN – The running back will pull the ball.

Counter
Using Formations and Motions

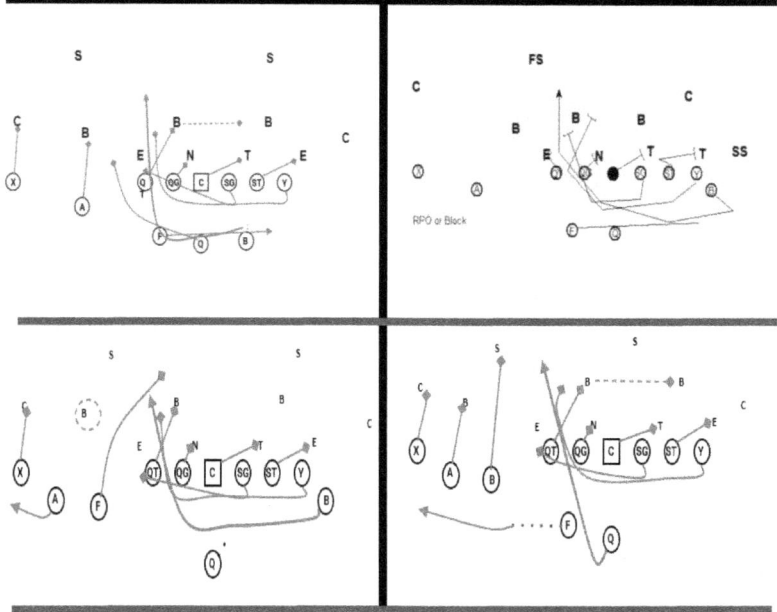

Once our players understand the **concept**, here are a few examples of using formations, so the play appears different to a defense.

The bottom left box shows an example from empty. The QB can throw the "peak", or hand the ball off to the running back.

The bottom right box shows an example of a quick motion RPO. The QB can throw the ball on the screen or simply run the counter himself.

Counter
Using Formations and Motions

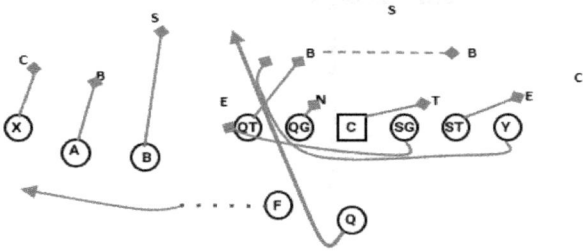

In this example, the offensive line continues to block for "counter", but the quick motion gives a screen into quads as a pre-snap option. If the defense does shift to take the screen away, the QB simply runs the counter.

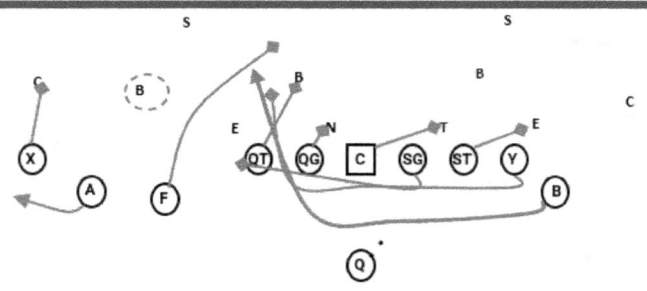

In this example, the QB has a post-snap RPO. He reads the linebacker. If the linebacker fits on the run, he throws the "peak" or "spot" route in the window. If the linebacker plays the passing window, the QB hands the ball off to the wingback.

Counter
RPOs to tag with Counter

Blue-Counter-Bubble
Bubble Pre-snap

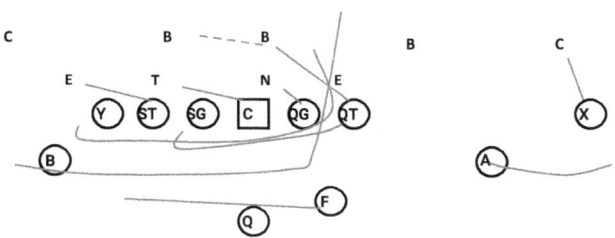

A very simple pre-snap read for the QB. This also works well against teams playing man-to-man to draw out the defense.

Red-Empty-Counter-2 Bubble
Q read OLB first bubble, then can shuffle if pressure. F crack second level defender. X blocks #1

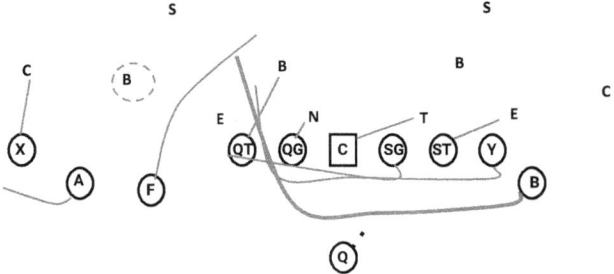

This is a post snap read for the QB. His eyes should go to the overhang defender. If he expands, hand it off. If he reads the run, throw the bubble.

Counter
RPOs to tag with Counter

Red-Empty-Flop-Counter-Fast
Q pre-snap Fast screen. Post-snap read 9 tech. F blocks most dangerous

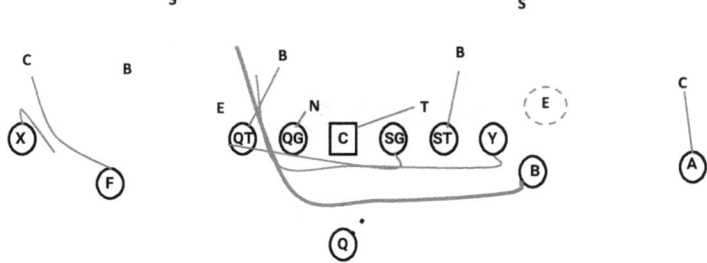

This is a pre-snap and post-snap RPO. The QB can throw the fast screen if he likes it pre-snap. Or he will read the Backside player on counter to pull and run the ball.

Red-Empty-Counter-Bubble
Bubble Pre-snap

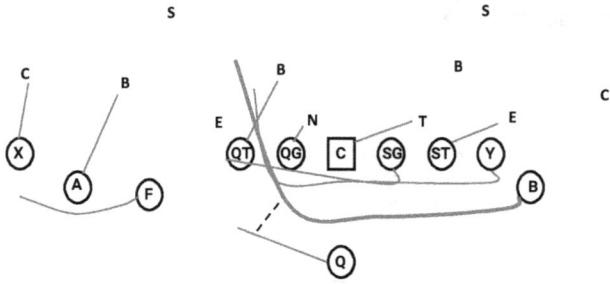

This is a pre-snap look for the QB. He can take the bubble if he likes the numbers or hand the ball off to the back on counter.

Counter
The "Blend"

Red-Strong-Flop-Counter-Shuffle

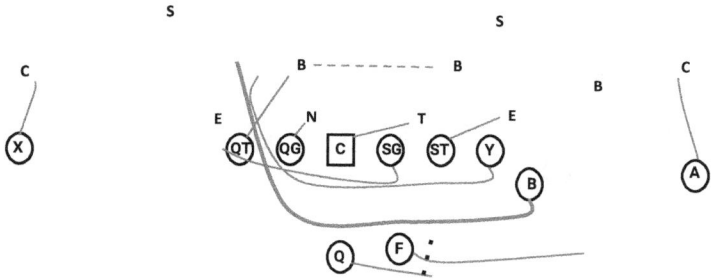

Counter is another **concept** that can look very different to a defense. Through the use of formations alone, it can become difficult for a defense to fit. In each of the examples listed, it has always followed the same blocking rules, although using the tags would be useful at any time. Once the players understand the **concept**, the adjustments become simple.

From a shuffle pass, to a 3-part RPO, the blocking scheme does not change. This allows for the **concept** to be run from any look the offense wants to use. It can be dressed up even more by using the QB as the runner in an empty look, or off of Jet-Motion.

Counter
The "Blend"

Red-Lion-Fly-Q Counter-Bubble
Bubble Pre-snap

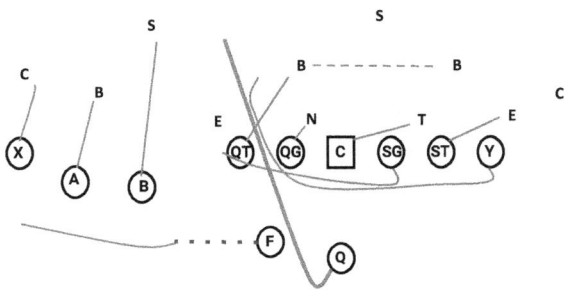

This is a simple way to force the hand of the defense by sending a quick motion and blending it with a pre-snap RPO.

The QB can throw the ball if the defense does not move, or he runs the ball if they go with the motion.

It keeps the integrity of the play, but must be played completely differently by the back end of the defense as they are now seeing a quads look away from the tight end.

Simple for the offense, but difficult for a defense.

Counter
If-Then

IF the defense is squeezing hard on the backside

THEN

1) We will read the backside squeezing player from an empty set. If he squeezes, the QB pulls the ball and runs to the voided space.

1) We can "Stay" call our TE and only pull our Guard.

1) We will "Switch" call and pull Guard/Tackle and leave the TE home.

The goal is to provide answers to when teams attempt to read the blocking scheme.

Counter
If-Then

IF the defense is squeezing hard on the play side and condensing the hole

THEN

1) We will "log" with the pulling guard and wrap the TE wider.

1) We will "lock" the play side tackle on the 5-technique and double wrap our pulling players.

1) We will run an RPO play side to occupy the overhang player.

In short we want to have 2-3 answers to a play side issue. By logging the squeezing player we are able to hit counter wider and exploit the technique. If that does not work, we generally will attempt to base him out with a bigger player in our tackle and wrap underneath him.

If the issue is a force player, we will run a play side RPO and read him pre or post-snap.

If you would like more depth on the counter, there are multiple materials available at FBCoachsimpson.com.

Counter

Counter is another **concept** that can look very different to a defense. Through the use of formations alone it can become difficult for a defense to fit. In each of the examples listed, it has always followed the same blocking rules, although using the tags would be useful at any time. Once the players understand the **concept**, the adjustments become simple.

From a shuffle pass, to a 3-part RPO, the blocking scheme does not change. This allows for the **concept** to be run from any look the offense wants to use. It can be dressed up even more, by using the QB as the runner in an empty look, or off of Jet-Motion. This can even be run with the running back.

The RPO helps to protect the run game as well. When it is all "blended" together it makes one "play look like many". Not only is counter its own separate **concept**, but it plays well as an actual "counter" to Buck. By putting these two **concepts** in the playbook, the offense is protecting the system from all the looks a defense may use in a game. Another example of the If-Then philosophy.

CHAPTER 8

PASS GAME SECTION

-ROLLOUT
-PLAY ACTION
-SCREENS

SNAG

Snag

Snag is not a unique play for many offenses. It is a staple in the passing game and can be utilized in most offenses, and is universally taught similar to how we teach it. The base **concept** is to have a corner that stretches the defense vertically, an intermediate curl/slant/dig route and a chute/bubble route, so the defense is challenged on three levels. If taught well, the **concept** has built in adjustments against zone or man-to-man. For example: the curl may turn into a slant or dig if the defense plays man.

The way offenses are able to get into this **concept** with formations, shifts and motions, as well as use multiple "tags" to change which receiver runs which route, is what can make it more difficult to defend.

Here is the base **concept** out of a 3 x 1 look for an offense.

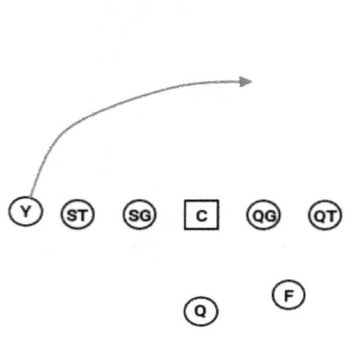 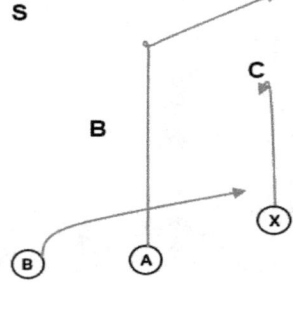

Snag

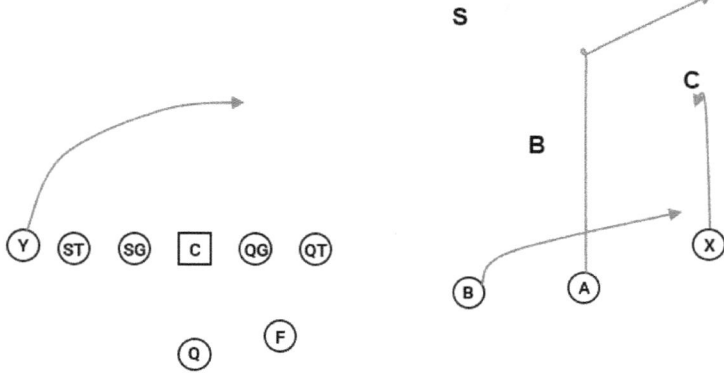

Position	Assignment
X	7-10 yard comeback – converts to slant if covered
A	Corner Route
F	Pass Pro
Y	Drag/Post Route
B	Chute Route – Can also be a bubble route
QT	Pass Pro
QG	Pass Pro
C	Pass Pro
SG	Pass Pro
ST	Pass Pro
Q	Read #1 outside DB – if he sits throw corner, if he drops read #2 Defensive Player

Snag
Using Formations and Motions

Squeeze-Bus-Snag
X outside release to 12 yards
A push to 7 then front pylon

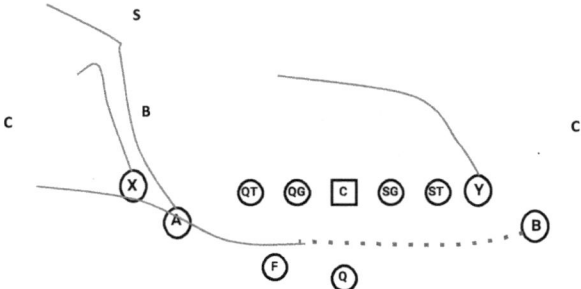

Bunch-Snag
A will work inside and then break for the corner
X runs the curl/slant
B runs inside and then pushes back to the chute

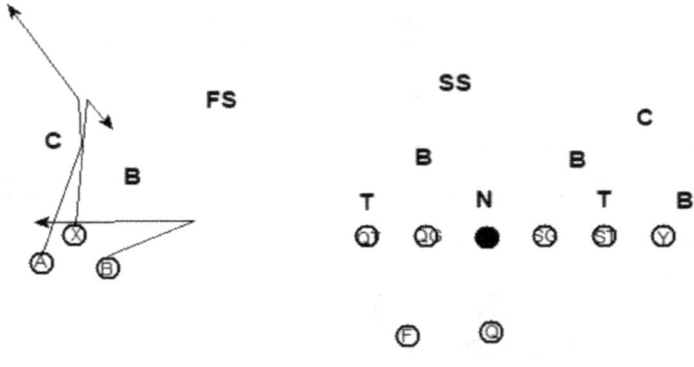

Using Formations

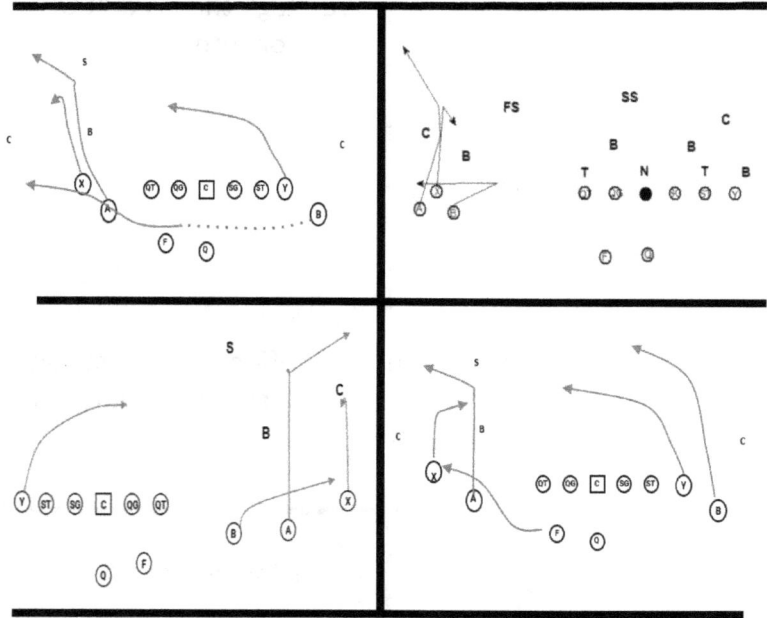

Snag can be run through multiple formations, but it does require 3 receivers to run the **concept**. One must run a corner route, one an intermediate route and one a route into the flats. How an offense chooses to get those receivers into the **concept** is what can make the play different.

From using motion to bunch formations, the concept never changes, but the routes will have to adjust. To a defense it seems complicated, but to an offense it is the same **concept**.

"Tags"

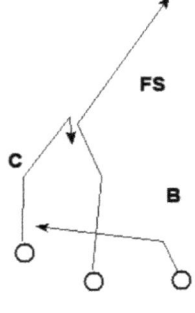

We "tag" this as a "COP" route or corner-post.

This is usually run from our offense against an aggressive safety, or if we like the matchup with our slot receiver against the safety.

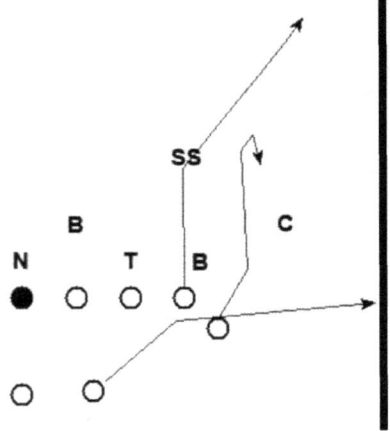

This is "snag-strong".

It is the same **concept**, run to a condensed set with a Tight-End and H-Back involving a running back. The read does not change for the Quarterback.

This is preferred against a Cover-2 look to a condensed set.

"Tags"

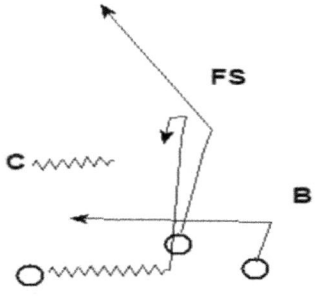

This is what we call "Patriot" motion into a bunch set.

Concept does not change, nor does the read.

This is an easy motion to use to help against man-to-man coverage or to help a Receiver get off of press coverage. It also creates more space for the corner route to come open.

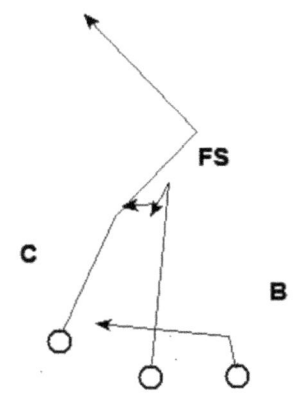

This tag is "Switch" for us. We simply switch the roles of our "X" and "A" Receivers.

We keep the same read for the Quarterback as the integrity of the **concept** is still in place.

This is another way to give a defensive team a different look, but run the same **concept**. The "switch" does create more space for the corner route as well.

Specials

Motion-Snag-X throwback
X work 7-10 and then across gaining depth to 15-20
Can cheat alignment tighter to line of scrimmage

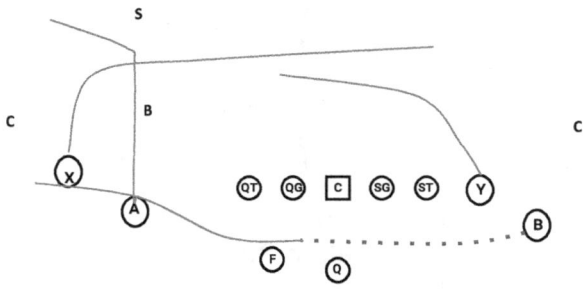

Motion-Snag-A throwback
A works 7-10 and then across gaining depth to 15-20

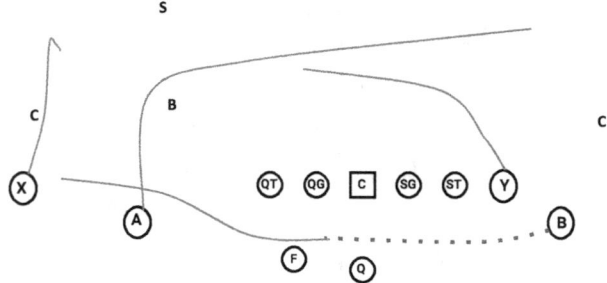

If-Then

IF the defense is playing zone

THEN
The "X" route converts to a comeback/curl

The offense should be able to read the corner to outside backer for the progression

The route will be better from a 3 x 1 set (numbers advantage)

IF the defense is playing man-to-man

THEN
The "X" route will convert to a slant/dig depending on leverage

The offense will often throw the corner route

Bunch formations will help with releases and confusion

Use motion or involve the running back into the scheme

Snag

Snag is a widely run concept. Hopefully, this will show some of the theory behind teaching routes as adjustable based on the defense's coverage. It is also difficult as an offense begins to run the same concept from different formations or by "switching" routes of receivers.

The goal is to keep the **concept** simple for your players, while dressing it up to confuse a defense. You are also building in answers to potential problems the **concept** must be able to handle. You are using the same **concept**, but giving adjustments to handle multiple looks or create the desired matchup.

WAGGLE

Waggle

Waggle is a staple of the Wing T offense, but is also seen in many other offensive systems. As with all the other **concepts** in this book, simply look at this **concept** as an example that I am using to illustrate a play action pass. There are also other route combinations that could be tagged into waggle in an offensive system. The goal is simply to show how to use a play action pass **concept** and dress it up.

For this example, waggle is taught as a play action, boot away from the run action. It is drawn below. The quarterback progression for us is:

Pressure – throw the angle route

Time to throw – check the deep comeback, come back to drag

Backside – Read the backside safety for dig/post concept

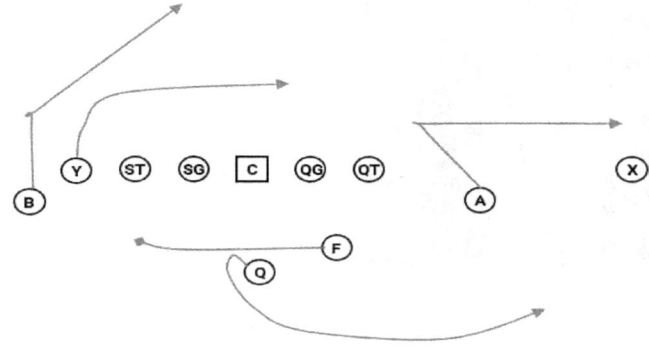

Waggle

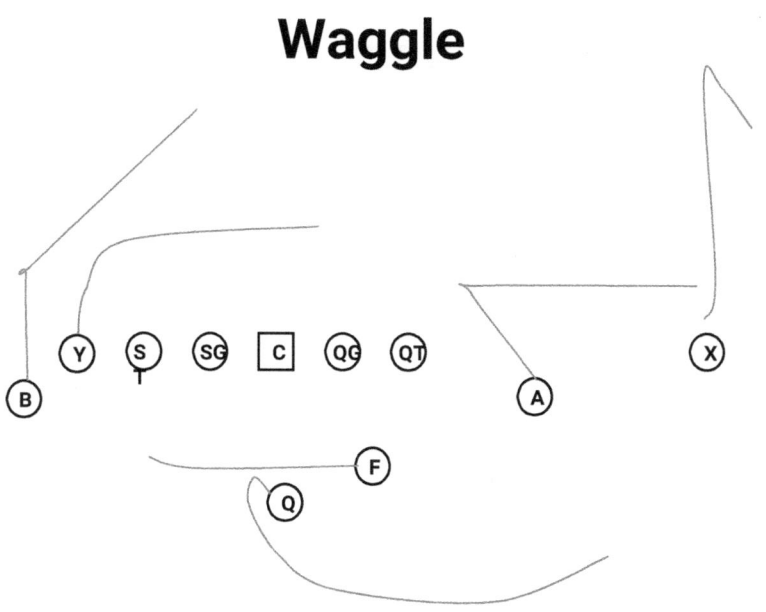

Position	Assignment
X	15-yard come-back route
A	Whip Route
F	Fake Buck – Block Edge
Y	Drag Route
B	Post-Over Safety Route
QT	Roll Out Protection
QG	Roll Out Protection
C	Roll Out Protection
SG	Roll Out Protection
ST	Roll Out Protection
Q	Fake Buck – Roll out

Waggle

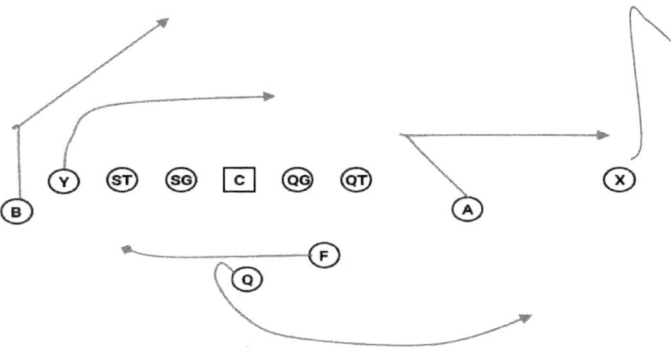

Traditional "waggle" look from an offense. The line would protect for boot.

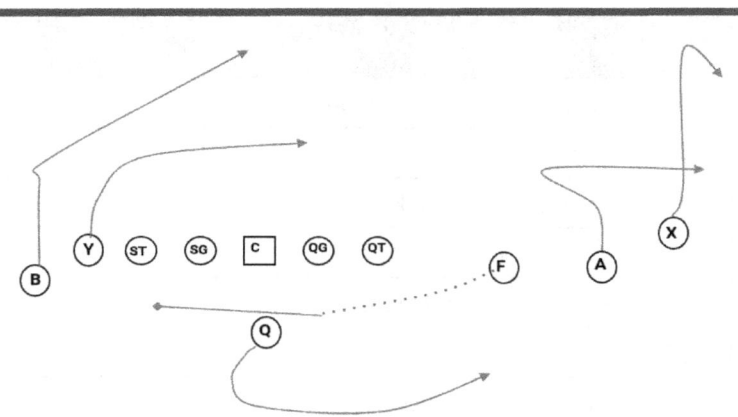

This is the exact same **concept** run the same way. The only change is motioning from an Empty set. While this is simple for the offense, it can create issues for the defense as they must adjust to: Empty, Motion and a Boot Pass.

Using Formations

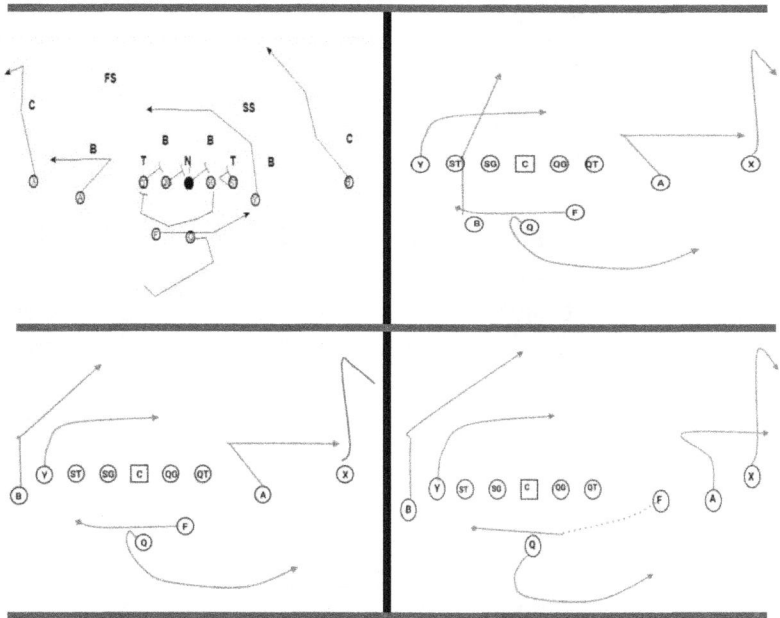

The goal of formations should be to create an advantage for the offense. Here are four examples of the same **concept** run from different formations. Each can create a different advantage for the offense based on how a defense lines up to the formation.

Formations

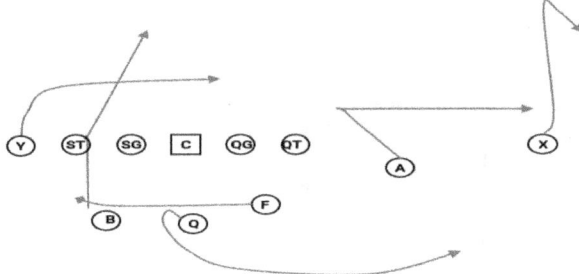

In this example the offense is in a 2-back set. The "B" understands he will end up on a post from the backfield if he has been taught the **concept** well. The potential advantage would be almost a "throwback" look to teams that may play man-to-man against a Tight-End look. The idea would be to get the "B" running against a linebacker.

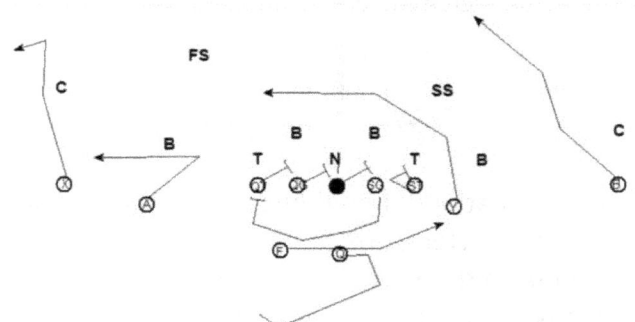

In this example the offense is running "waggle" from a 20 personnel grouping. The **concept** does not change, but it can cause more stress on the defense as the offense has a more vertical threat on the backside.

Play Options

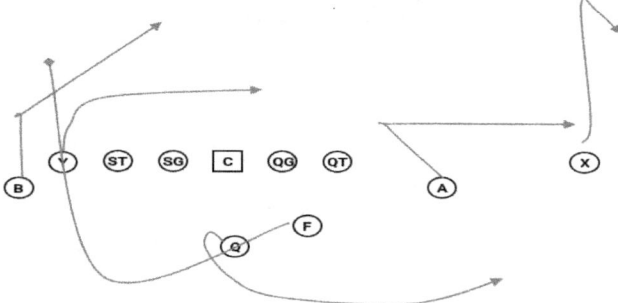

While any route can be tagged and adjusted, here is an example of "waggle" with a "wheel route" by the running back. It is a great shot play or against a man-to-man defensive team.

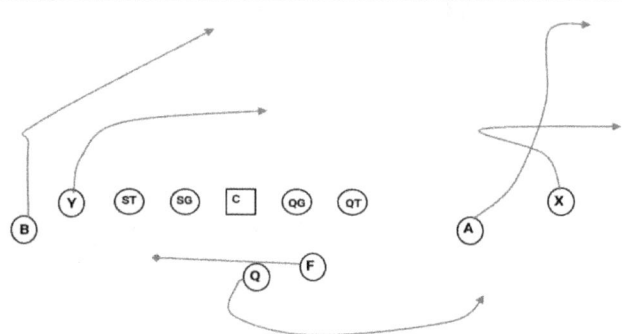

This is a "switch" call with "waggle". It tells the "X" and "A" to switch responsibilities or routes. Thus the "X" is now running a whip route and the "A" is running a deep out route.

Waggle
The "Blend"

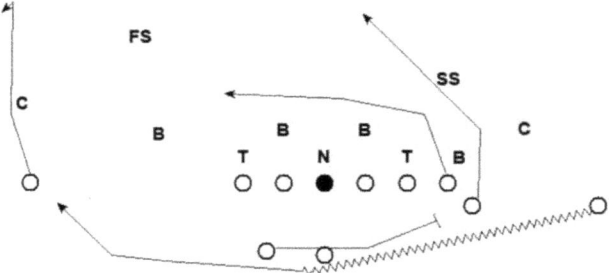

This is the same **concept** with a motion across the formation and a bubble route instead of a whip route. It is a great adjustment against man-to-man, or if the defense is overloading the trips look.

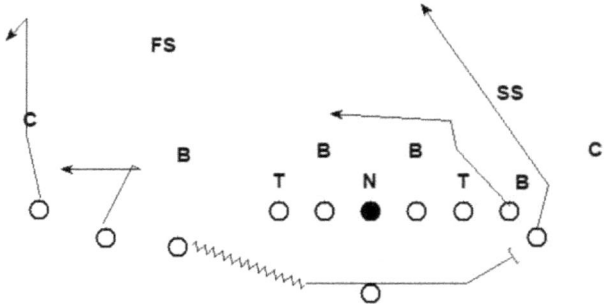

Waggle from an Empty look. It is simple enough, but can cause a better look for the offense with minimal practice time.

If-Then

IF – The defense is overplaying the run to the strong side

THEN –

Waggle should be a go-to play.

The TE/Wing will more than likely be open on the backside

IF – If the defense is reading the line in the box

THEN –

Consider pulling a lineman to the run game and running more of a "naked" boot

Waggle

Waggle is a very common play for many offenses. Most may refer to this as "boot" or a play action boot pass. The routes may change on the play-side and that is fine, but the **concept** remains the same. Faking the run and "booting" the quarterback the opposite direction.

If seen as a **concept**, the possibilities with these types of **concepts** are endless. The entire goal is to use the run action to create space for the wide receivers. At the minimum this should create a 1-on-1 matchup. If done correctly, it may lead to wide open players.

SCREENS

Now Screen

More than likely every offense has a version of a "Now" or "Fast" screen attached. Some will use this **concept** as an RPO, while others may have their line involved and not choose to make a read. How ever the **concept** is used, it can be adapted and built upon to make it more effective.

We teach the **concept** from the outside-in with the ability to throw a "Now" screen to any Receiver that is split out.

The base blocking rules for our system are to block the first outside defensive player OR most dangerous threat. For example: if the corner in this set were to bail on the snap, we would want our eyes to come inside.

Blocking Rules

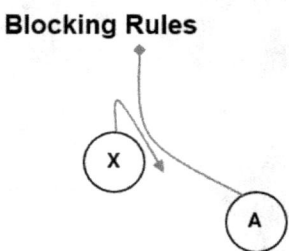

Now Screen

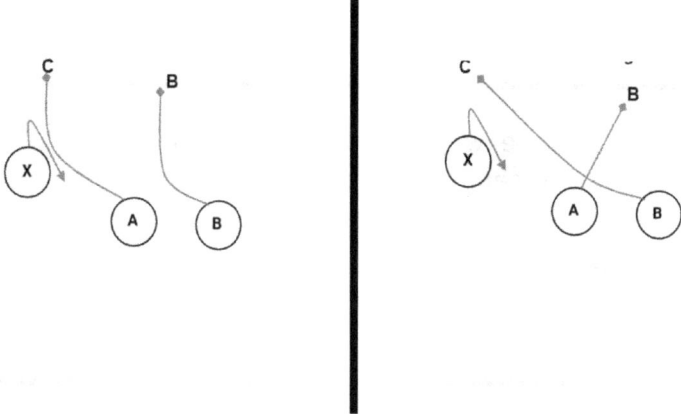

Position	Assignment
X	Now Screen
A	Block #1 or MDT (example 1) -- Crack #2 (example 2)
B	Block #2 or MDT (example 1 – Block #1 (example 2)

Here are two examples of running a "Now" screen to a trips look.

In the first example we teach it the base way – with each Receiver blocking the first defender outside.

In the second example we are "X" blocking the defense.

Flavors of Now

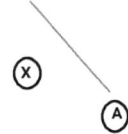

Base way we would teach a "Now" screen to a twins look.

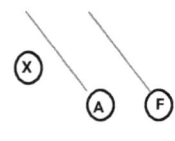

Base way we would teach a "Now" screen to a trips look.

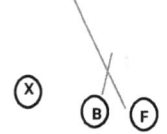

Running a "Now" screen with an "X" block tag.

While this **concept** can be used for "Now" screens in any set, this should give a general idea of how we teach the base **concept**.

Using Motion

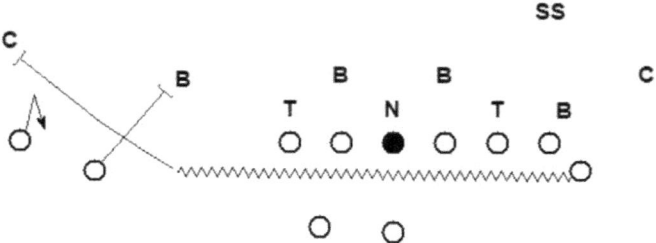

This is still the "Now" screen. The offense is simply motioning to a trips look to create a numbers advantage. The **concept** does not change – this would be an "X" block from motion.

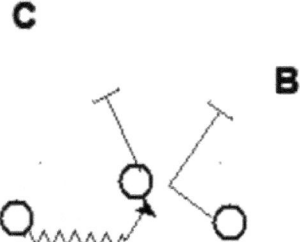

This is an example of another use of motion to create an advantage. While it does not help with the numbers, it does create an advantage by forming a "bunch" look and making the blocking much easier for the receivers.

"Divorced" Concepts

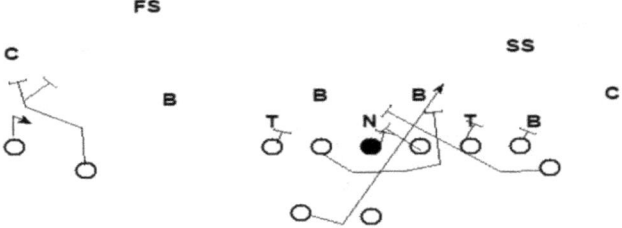

In many offenses, including my own, "Now" screens are paired with a run. They can be run as "divorced" **concepts**. They each operate at the same time, but are independent of each other. In this example the quarterback can take the screen or hand the ball off for ISO.

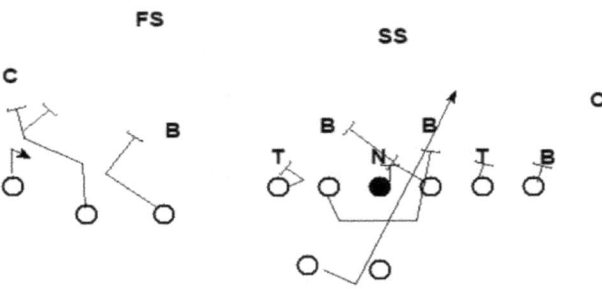

This is the same "divorced" **concepts**, but in a trips set. The line and running back are running ISO, but the trips are working a "Now" screen. The **concepts** are independent from each other.

Using RPOs

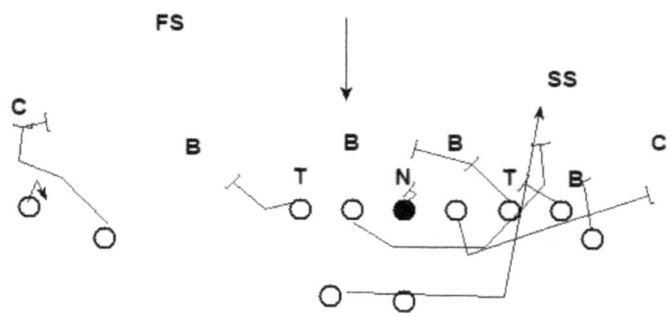

This is a post-snap RPO. The quarterback can throw the pre-snap "Now" screen, or he can read it out and pull the ball to run, or flip the ball out late. It is dependent on the backside 4I and linebacker. If he pulls and feels pressure, he can throw the screen late.

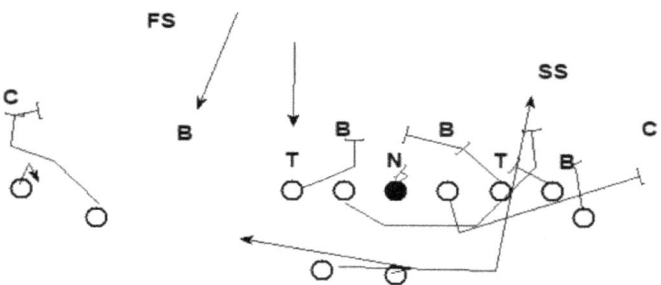

This is another flavor of a quarterback read. He does have the option to throw the "Now" screen, or can read the play out and throw the screen later. This is basically triple option football from the shotgun.

If-Then

IF – The Defense is playing off coverage at corner

THEN –

Slot should be blocking the "Most Dangerous Threat" which would turn into the Linebacker or Safety rolling down

---

IF – The Defense is playing a hard cover 2 look

THEN –

The offense should consider throwing a now screen to #2 WR

The offense can align in trips to gain a blocker if needed and throw the now screen to #2

CONCLUSION

Conclusion

"The greatest compliment a coach can get from another coach around the league is, 'Hey, your guys play hard. They're tough.' "
Sean McDermott

Calling plays and having a great scheme is very important. I believe as a coach it is our duty to our players to always give them the best opportunity to win the game by constantly studying the game and evolving our offensive system each season. It is my hope that this book gave you some ideas in which to think about teaching football through **concepts.**

However, the best designed offensive, or defensive, system does not matter if the culture of the program is not right. Do the players believe in each other? Do they believe and understand the scheme? Do they understand that effort and intensity will always beat scheme?

Study scheme as much as possible, but do not forget that coaching football has always been about relationships. It is my hope that this book may have given you a few ideas about how to see the offensive or defensive side of the ball. X's and O's do matter, and they can help a team win games, but great coaches recognize that relationships and motivation are much more important. I believe it takes both scheme and a great culture, and ultimately successful teams do well at both.

Conclusion

While I used plays that are specific to my offensive system, I am hopeful that these ideas would apply to any offensive system. Teams have been successful with run heavy systems, pass heavy systems, spread offenses and full-house backfields. The goal is to put your athletes in the best position to win.

To do this, not only must a coach find a system that fits his personnel, but he must also understand the offense so well, that making adjustments to each concept becomes almost second nature. This can only be done with experience and tremendous amounts of time being invested in learning the why to his offensive system.

We show our athletes that we care about them, and are constantly striving to become better at giving them tools to be successful on the field. More importantly, make sure you are doing your best for your athletes off the field.

If I can do anything for you please do not hesitate to call, text or email. Coaches are key to raising the next generation, and I want to do my best to help serve them. You are leaving an impact on more people that you can imagine. Make it a great one.

"Nobody cares how much you know, until they know how much you care."
Theodore Roosevelt

ABOUT THE AUTHOR

About the Author

Coach Simpson has served at three schools as the Head Football Coach: Searcy High School, a 6A school in Arkansas in 2020. Before Searcy, he was the Head Football Coach at Southside Charter. Taking over a program that had won eight games in five seasons and had been on a 20+ game losing streak, Simpson led Southside to the playoffs for four-consecutive seasons and won two conference titles in the last three seasons. For his efforts, he was named 4A-2 Conference Coach of the Year (2017), named as a finalist for Hooten's Coach of the Year (2017) and has been the All-Star Nominee for the 4A-2 (2016 and 2019). He was also selected to coach in the 1st FCA Texas-Arkansas All-Star Showdown (2021). Simpson's teams have qualified for the playoffs the past 5 consecutive seasons.

Coach Simpson wrote his first book in 2019. *Find A Way: What I Wish I'd Known When I Became A Head Football Coach*, and he has been a three-time best seller on Amazon in several categories. He has released 10 other books.

His offense has now run across the globe in not only the United States, but also in South America, Africa, Japan, Europe and Australia. He has helped to install the Gun-T system in many schools over the past 2-years.

About the Author

Simpson has also raised over $1.5 million for Southside and has overseen several major facility projects including: New Field Turf, Expansion to Fieldhouse, Expansion to the school's home bleachers, and the addition of a press box and a new video-board.

Prior to coming to Southside, Simpson took over as Head Coach at Alabama Christian Academy in Montgomery, Alabama. During his tenure there, Simpson took over a team that had been 4-18 and led them to their first home playoff game in over 20 years. For his efforts he was named Montgomery Advertisers' All-Metro Coach of the Year as well as being voted 4A Region 2 Coach of the Year (2010).

Simpson also served as the head track coach at ACA and led his teams to multiple top 10 finishes in 4A.

Simpson began his coaching career at Madison Academy, in Huntsville, Alabama. He served as a junior high basketball and football coach, before working into a varsity coaching role in football. He graduated from Harding University in 2003. He is married to Jamey and has three children: Avery, Braden and Bennett. The couple was married in 2001 after meeting at Harding University.

About the Author

Simpson's Books

Find A Way
Coaching Football Like A Basketball Coach
Training Athletes Beyond The Game
Athletic Fundraising
Team Theme Book

Gun T System Books

Gun T Playbook
Gun T 2.0
Gun T Organizational Manual
Gun T Offensive Line Manual
Gun T Youth Manual

Defensive Books

34 Fit and Swarm Overview

www.ingramcontent.com/pod-product-compliance
Lightning Source LLC
Chambersburg PA
CBHW072135160426
43197CB00012B/2119